INTERVENTION FOR SLOW LEARNERS

INTERVENTION FOR SLOW LEARNERS

By

Dr. R. Ramar
Headmaster
S.S.H.N. Higher Secondary School
Muhavur–626 111
Tamil Nadu

SONALI PUBLICATIONS
NEW DELHI-110002

Edition : 2021

ISBN 81-88836-43-5

Published by

SONALI PUBLICATIONS
4228/1, Ansari Road,
New Delhi-110 002 (India)
Phone: 23279245 • Fax: 91-11-23253475

Printed at:
Navya Digital, Delhi - 110092

Preface

My earnest concern over the growing number of slow learners at all levels of education pushed me on to venture into the untrodden area. This study is a pioneer work, perhaps the first of its kind in Indian context, since there is no study on slow learners in the Survey Books of Buch. In a country like India where human resource is abundant but human resource development is not adequate, studies of this type are warranted to optimise human resource development which will, in turn, tell upon ultimate national development.

The first chapter focuses on the concept of slow learners and the need for combating slow learning to ensure adequate human resource development. The second chapter enumerates the related literature reviewed to gain an insight into the theoretical groundings and practical perspectives. This chapter highlights the landmarks achieved and the lapses and pitfalls that are still existing and the problems that require immediate attention. The third chapter delineates the conceptual framework and the fourth one presents the experimental design and the scientific methodology applied in the study. The fifth chapter deals with results and discussions. It lists out the findings that strengthen earlier findings and the findings that need to be strengthened in future works. The last chapter provides the summary, implications of the study for educational practitioners and exhaustive suggestions for further research.

This book will be of immense use for the research scholars since it provides them with the required direction in selection and experimentation of the study. This book will serve as a very useful Handbook for educational practitioners at all levels of our educational system for it gives them vital information regarding concept and causes of slow learning. Also, it enumerates the characteristics of slow learners and the procedures to identify slow learners. Also, the book provides useful guidelines as to how to develop modules and multimedia packages. This book is a practical book for the students of B.Ed., M.Ed., and M.Phil courses. It is my sincere hope that this book will get wide acclaim from students and scholars as well as from preceptors at all levels of our educational system.

I sincerely thank M/s Sonali Publications, New Delhi for the keen interest they envinced in publishing this book and for the care they took to add look and charm to the book.

R. Ramar

Acknowledgements

I express my deep sense of gratitude to Dr. G. Lokanadha Reddy, Senior Lecturer in Adult and Non-formal Education, Department of Education, Alagappa University, Karaikudi for his valuable guidance and encouragement throughout the period of the present investigation.

I am highly indebted to Dr. S. Mohan, Professor and Head, Department of Education, Alagappa University, Karaikudi for providing necessary facilities in the department to carry out the present investigation. Further, I would like to record my special thanks to him for the inspirations that he imbibed in me from time to time during the period of investigation.

I am very much thankful to Dr. P. Prema, Dr. R. Krishnaraj, Shri P. Paul Devanesan and other non-teaching staff of the Department of Education, Alagappa University, Karaikudi for their assistance from time to time to accomplish this task.

I am highly indebted to Dr. Venkataiah, Dean, Faculty of Education, University of Mysore, Mysore and Dr. Padmanabaiah, Professor and Head, Department of Education, S.V. University, Tirupathi for their critical comments and feed back which added to the refinement of research design and methodology.

Also, my profound thanks are due to Dr. Sathyavathi, Professor and Head, Department of Education, Sri Padmavathi Mahila Viswa Vidhyalaym, Tirupathi and Dr. Kusuma, Senior Lecturer of the same department whose constructive suggestions added to the enrichment of the research report.

I would like to thank all the panel experts, especially Dr. Sivasubramanian. Principal, ANJA College, Sivakasi and

Dr. Sanjeevi Raja, Senior Lecturer, Department of Physics, Alagappa University, Karaikudi for reviewing the modules and multimedia packages and for providing practical suggestions for perfection.

My sincere thanks are due to my beloved staff members Messrs M. Paramasivam, P.G. Teacher (History), P. Janakkumar, P.G. Teacher (English), R. Thalaimalai, P.G. Teacher (Botany), R. Natarajan, P.G. Teacher (Physics), M.V. Kannan, P.G. Teacher (Chemistry) and K. Kannan, P.G. Teacher (Maths) for their immense contributions to the development of modules and multimedia packages.

I also wish to thank the proprietor of Sharp Video Vision, Rajapalayam for his unflinching co-operation in video shooting and editing.

I am very grateful to computer experts Er. K. Sridhar, M.E., Er. K. Ramasubramanian, B.E., and Shri K. Kannan, proprietor to KKR Computer Centre, Muhavur for their commitment and assistance in development of software for CAI and in bringing out the computer print. The end product would not have been feasible without such commitment and interest in the project.

I am highly indebted to the subjects of the study for extending their cooperation to complete this work.

(R. RAMAR)

CONTENTS

1

INTRODUCTION

CONCEPT, MEANING AND DEFINITION OF HUMAN RESOURCE DEVELOPMENT

It is a well known fact that a nation's economic growth as well as national development is very much determined by the resources available in that country. There are various resources such as water resource, land resource, mineral resource etc., which all serve as vital determinants of a country's ultimate development.

The fundamental factors that make for the national development and economic growth are non-economic and non-materialistic in character. It is the spirit that itself builds the body. Some countries of the world have experienced a rapid rise in income and living standards while others continue to stagnate at the lowest rung of the ladder. The spirit has been the guiding factor of national development in all the developed countries.

The size and quality of the people; the size and efficiency of the labour force and the serving cadres, the health, intelligence and diligence of the people; the sense of discipline, character and the spirit of co-operation of the people etc. are the factors that facilitate national development. But, these are obviously the outcomes of human resource development. Though there exist various resources such as water resource, land resource, forest resource, energy resource, human resource etc., which all serve as vital determinants of a country's ultimate development, the resource that decisively determines the economic growth and national development of a country is invariably the human resource.

Most of the backward countries are backward not because of inadequate supply of physical and financial resources but because of acute shortage of skilled personnel and technicians. Education promotes and develops an openness of mind, tolerance, co-operation, ability to adjust to the changes. Above all, it lays stress on the qualities of courage and endurance and encourages a vigorous and relentless pursuit of truth and free enquiry. Education enhances the understanding of the behaviour of interrelationships among the tangible and the intangible phenomena surrounding and imparts skill to translate the knowledge into action and make the most beneficial use of them. These developments in the human resources which may be termed as human capital, contribute much more to economic growth and national development than physical capital (A.K. Ghosh, 1996).

Quality of population depends upon its education, health, vigour, training, morale etc. Provision of better education, medical facilities and training opportunities etc., are tantamount to investment in human capital, as distinguished from investment in matérial capital like machines, tools etc. It has been estimated that the return, in terms of output, has been as high or even higher from human capital than from an equal investment in real capital. This conclusion is becoming increasingly valid with the advancement of technology and sophistication in products. The educated, trained and alert labour force is very essential to man the complicated machines, and to manage the complex economic life of growing economies.

While a natural resource is anything found by man in his natural environment that he may in some way utilise for his own benefit, human resources are the human beings whose contribution society can use for different purposes. The worker in a factory is an example of a human resource. Human resource refers to the various service cadres. Here, every one is unique in his own sphere and his contribution can not be ignored. A farmer, carpenter, cobbler, plumber, mason, potter, a government servant etc. are the indispensable as well as integral constituents of human resources.

Human resource development refers to the qualitative improvement of the labour forces and the service cadres by way of providing better education, proper training and ensuring good health which will, ultimately, tell upon their performance. Human resource development means preparing individuals So as to make them evince utmost manifestation and efficient application of potentials in the task assigned or undertaken. Where there is a good degree of human resource development, there will be invariably all round development for it is the human resource development that gears up the national development.

RELATIONSHIP BETWEEN HUMAN RESOURCE DEVELOPMENT AND NATIONAL DEVELOPMENT

Though there are various resources which serve as determinants of economic growth and ultimate national development, it is the human resource that stands foremost and it is the human resource which can alone ensure the effective utilisation of other resources. Hence, human resource development is the only key to national development and economic growth. It is the nucleus of economic growth. It is the king-pin of development. It is the salt of nationalism which sustains the spirit of patriotism and belongingness.

For instance, Japan which was reduced to a heap of ashes at the end of second world-war rose from the ruins to make a mighty nation. It was possible only because of the tremendous human resource development that took place in Japan in the post war period. It is a nation that has no natural resources. Oil, natural gas and coal are only scarcely found. Cotton does not grow there. How has it been possible for Japan then to build again? The answer is the will and work of its great people.

Japan vies today with other nations of the world. Its eminence in the field of electronics has been nothing short of a miracle. From cameras, calculators and digital watches to computers and robots—everything is made in Japan. They are the best sellers in the world market. They could achieve this target from the heap of ashes because the Japanese are the world's most educated people today. Their system of education is rigorous.

For a country struggling to achieve higher levels of growth, the only great asset can be the various labour forces and the service cadres. Swiss people have made up their deficiency of natural resources by their diligence and enterprise. As already mentioned, the secret of Japan's astounding success in the economic field in the years following the end of the second world war lies in the diligence, enterprise, thriftiness, sense of discipline and the spirit of patriotism of the Japanese people.

According to economists, the three fundamental factors inducing economic growth and accelerating national development are labour, capital and technology. A well trained labour force and a well devised technology are the by products of human resource development and the effective utilisation of the capital depends on these two factors *i.e.,* labour and technology and, in turn, capital remains a must for human resource development.

We can never conceive of a plan to gear up national development without human resources. Hence, the need for human resource development. Aiming at national development without ensuring human resource development is meaningless. But ensuring human resource development is more easily said than done. It is a process with many bottlenecks but the problems are not unsurmountable.

PROBLEMS IN HUMAN RESOURCE DEVELOPMENT

The problems that we encounter and that we have to surmount are numerous and varied in India. India is a land known for natural resources. There is no dearth of natural resources. Also, there is human resource in abundance. In human resource, India stands next to our neighbour China only. But, in terms of human resource development or developed human resources, we are nowhere in the rank and we pitiably remain in the lower rung of the ladder. There are various omissions and commissions that hinder or retard human resource development in India.

There is no 100 per cent enforcement of compulsory education. People living from hand to mouth still prefer to send their children for daily labour. In the school also, most of the pedagogues fail to motivate the students and to imbibe in them the spirit of patriotism and the feeling of brotherhood and belongingness. Also, they do not cultivate properly sense of discipline and sense of tolerance.

At higher level, our educational system is neither life oriented nor job oriented. Vocational education is only for name sake. Studies without practical approach are quite common. Institutions do not have the adequate infrastructure. Mushroom growth of technical institutes is a good example for this. There is lack of proper training and no place for work experience. Field trip is not properly arranged and effectively used. Also, our educational system lays stress on memorisation only, not on application of skill and knowledge.

Also, there has been a lot of discussion on reaching and utilising the research findings at the field level. Useful work has been done in this direction particularly in the agricultural and medical sciences. But the chasm between researchers and practitioners still remains in education which is a vital determinant of human resource development and ultimately national development. Nothing seems to percolate down to the classroom level inspite of the plethora of researches going on at the university level and those done by research and training organisations. The research findings intended to ensure human resource development by means of promoting better teaching learning process usually find themselves adorning the shelves. They are seldom put into practice which is all the more needed in a developing country like India to bring about optimum human resource development.

Our educational system does not cater to the endowed and the ignored. There is lack of integrity and duty consciousness both among the teachers and the taught. Educational technology as a separate discipline has emerged only recently. Above all, there is no sufficient investment in human capital in India when compared with developed countries. It is possible to surmount the problems faced in human resource development by ensuring proper enforcement of compulsory education, adequate investment in human capital and by adopting proper methods and techniques for human resource development.

METHODS AND TECHNIQUES FOR HUMAN RESOURCE DEVELOPMENT

Government policy, implementation of government policy in spirit and letter, appropriate use of certain media and technology are the ways to ensure human resource development. Government and voluntary social action groups can join hands to alleviate the quality, skill and ability of the task force and the service cadres through education, health and economic activities. Also, the latter two depend on the proper acquisition of the former.

Method is a special form of procedure especially in any branch of mental activity whereas technique is a mode of artistic execution. Since education plays a pivotal role in human resource development, the magnitude of need for an effective method of instruction and training is immense. A method incorporating appropriate media and technology alone can ensure optimum instruction and training. Media and technology based instruction arouses the curiosity of the students, ignites and sustains the spark of interest and ensures mastery learning and long retention. When the teachers provide effective instruction and intensive training to the learners of various types and levels, they are bound to evince an ostent performance in the task assigned or undertaken. This is what is precisely meant by human resource development.

Also, the technique of instruction by the teacher plays a no smaller role in human resource development. Only resourceful people can make use of the resources locally available for the betterment of the society. It is more true so in case of the personnel involved in human resource development. When the teacher or the trainer lacks apt technique, it is not possible to aim at human resource development. But, by providing orientation, the teacher or the trainer can be trained up to sharpen his technique of instruction or training.

Even when the teacher or the trainer is knowledgeable about the method and adept at technique, he should have psychological understanding about the endowed and the ignored. They should devise their instruction or training in such a way that it should cater to both the endowed and the ignored. If either of them is neglected, it will not be possible to aim at or to bring about optimum human resource development because in India there are a large number of under achievers, low achievers and slow learners, who sheerly outnumber the endowed or gifted students.

CONCEPT, MEANING AND DEFINITION OF INDIVIDUAL DIFFERENCES

Each trait of an individual depends on his heredity and environment. Therefore, in order to know the individual, it is necessary to understand his heredity and environment. Here the question arises as to which of the two-heredity or environment is more important for the development of a person. One school wants to give the entire credit to heredity and the other school considers environment all important in an individual's development. There is a third school which says that an individual inherits physical traits like the colour of the hair, height, weight, full size and shape of the body from heredity and acquires mental traits like ability, memory etc., through learning or environment.

Evidently, both heredity and environment have their own important place in an individual's development. In a way, both heredity and environment are interdependent so far as an individual's development is concerned and neglecting any of the two will be fatal to his development. Due to these two operating factors individual differences are found in physical as well as mental aspects of the students. But in this study, the main focus is on the individual differences encountered in the intellectual development of students and also how to accommodate instruction to these individual differences.

The problem that plagues every teacher in every subject at every grade level is how to teach one lesson to a class that contains students with different skills and learning rates. Accommodating instruction to student differences is one of the most fundamental problems of education and often leads to politically and emotionally charged policies.

The problem of accommodating student differences is so important that many educationists have suggested that instruction be completely individualised so that students can work independently at their own rates. In the past twenty years, this point of view has led to the creation of individualised instructional programmes and computer assisted instruction. Simply speaking, individual difference refers to how the students differ from one another in a variety of ways, some important to instruction, some not.

Each of the many ways of accommodating student differences has its own benefits, but each introduces its own problems, which some times outweigh the benefits. Researches on various means of accommodating classroom instruction to student differences have been undertaken. However, before delving into the details, it will be apt to consider what student differences are and which of them the teachers must take into account.

Bases of Individual Differences

From their first day in a school, students differ. They differ on several obvious dimensions that are of little importance to instruction. But they also differ in cognitive abilities and learning rates, which are of great concern to educators.

Many students enter L.K.G. or First Standard knowing the alphabet and numbers upto ten, and some can already read a little; others lack these skills. As time goes on, initial differences between students tend to increase, so that by high school or higher secondary school, students may enter class with markedly different skills. As the students go higher and higher in the educational ladder, the existing chasm becomes wider and wider and it becomes a serious problem to the educator. For example, two Fourth-graders who differ by one grade equivalent in reading or mathematics performance are likely to differ by three grade equivalents by the twelfth grade (Coleman *et al.,* 1966).

Differences in prior learning create the most serious problem in instruction (Tobias, 1981; Como and Snow, 1986; Snow, 1986). For example, if a teacher presents a series of lessons on the discovery of America, it is of considerable importance to know how much students already know about the subject, how much they understand about the Renaissance in Europe, how well they can interpret maps and globes, and, at the most basic level, how well they can read. If students are quite diverse in these skills, then the teacher must somehow take this diversity into account when presenting the lesson.

Another student difference that teachers have to take into account is learning rate. Even if all students begin class at the same level, some are likely to learn more easily and rapidly than others. For example, a class learning a foreign language for the first time might begin with equal ignorance, but some students have an Ear for foreign languages that others lack, and some have greater motivation to learn a foreign language than others. For these and other reasons, some students will learn more rapidly than their class mates

A third difference that teachers should be aware of is learning style (Dunn and Dunn, 1998; Mossick, 1984; Carbo *et al.,* 1986). For example, some students learn best auditorily, some visually, some work best alone, others with peers, some need total silence to concentrate, others work well in a noisy room. Low Achievement in academic performance may be due to the aforesaid factors. The instructor should, therefore, take care of such bases of differences and accordingly devise his instruction so as to cater to individual differences, especially to low achievers, slow learners, etc.,

SLOW LEARNERS—CONCEPT, MEANING AND DEFINITION

Sometime a large segment of school going children present a serious problem to schools because they have limited scope for achievement. These pupils have intelligence quotients below 89 (Chintamani Kar, 1992) and they constitute about 18 per cent of the total school population. Their ability to deal with abstract and symbolic materials (*i.e.*, language, number and concepts) is very limited and their reasoning in practical situations is inferior to that of average students.

Slow learners differ from normal students in learning ability and learning rate. Normally, a slow learner does not stand out as very different from his class mates except that he is very slow on the uptake and he is often teased by the other boys because of his slowness. Research works (Tansley and R. Gulliford, 1962; Cleugh, 1957) reveal that the attention span of slow learners is relatively short. They are also unable to deal with relatively complex games or school assignments. They need much external stimulation and encouragement to do simple type of work.

Slow learners are those students who are unable to accomplish what is expected of their age group. Burt (1937) classifies them as students who are unable to cope with the work normally expected of their age group.

These students remain in the lowest rung of the ladder. They are found weak in almost all the subjects. They usually score less than 25 per cent in the tests.

Characteristics of Slow Learners

(i) Slow learners have limited cognitive capacity. Their IQ is low. They fail to cope with learning situation and to reason abstractly. Rational thinking becomes practically impossible. They have the capacity to succeed in rote learning. They evince interest in learning where relationships are clearly demonstrated. With regard to retentive memories, they require more practice and revision when compared with normal students.

(ii) Another distinguishing characteristic of slow learners is poor memory. It occurs due to lack of concentration (Burt, 1946). This weakness in what may be termed as long term memory hampers the educational progress of slow learners who need to go over the material more times before it is fixed in their minds, and more frequent revision is required to foil forgetting. The reason for their poor memory is that they are slow to perceive and use possible association. The efficiency of initial learning is important as well as actual retention and recall. These are all influenced by attitude, interest and emotional states.

(iii) Slow learners are marked for distraction and lack of concentration in classroom situation. This behaviour is also associated with poor motivation.

(iv) Inability to express ideas through language is another significant characteristic of slow learners. A slow learner lacks imagination and foresight. He finds it very difficult to foresee the consequences in future.

Causes of Slow Learning

The causes of slow learning are numerous but some important ones are discussed below:

(i) Poverty

In a developing country like India, poverty is deemed to be the primary cause of slow learning. Poverty affects children in two ways. It impairs children's health and it reduces their learning capacity. A child from a sophisticated family has a variety of avenues to explore and he gets plenty of materials to expand the dimensions of his existing knowledge. On the contrary, a child from an indigent family does not get enough opportunities to live a full life. However, poverty is not the sole cause of slow learning.

(ii) Intelligence of Family Members

Another potent factor of learning is the level of intelligence of parents as well as family members. It indirectly affects the learning of children. It is true that educated and intelligent parents can provide educational experiences and materials to their children according to their own intellectual level. But, the poor illiterate parents cannot take positive steps towards the upliftment of their children. Children coming from educated circles are not usually slow learners. Research evidences also confirm this fact.

(iii) Emotional Factors

Emotional factors contribute a lot towards the slow learning of the children. When a child comes to school, he brings his emotional world with him. Tensions and conflicts exercise a negative effect on learning of the child. So, the tensions at home, the relationship between siblings and parents themselves have an adverse effect on the child, not to mention the frustration which he sustains from his family and the external world. Very often children with autocratic home background are slow learners.

(iv) Personal Factors

Besides all these above factors, there are some personal factors which are also responsible for slow learning. These factors include long illness or long absence from school and lack of confidence in self. Children who lack self confidence are usually slow learners.

Notwithstanding, the aforesaid factors causing slow learning, the slow learners must be made to understand as much as they can of what they are learning, and then they need more repetition, revision and practice to ensure retention. It envisages a special intervening instructional strategy for slow learners which must encompass all the above factors.

NEED FOR INTERVENING INSTRUCTIONAL STRATEGY TO SURMOUNT SLOW LEARNING

Slow learner learns so slowly and unevenly because of his low intelligence and other causes that he is unable to cope satisfactorily with normal students. He is not, however so markedly different that his basic psychological, educational and social needs are in any way unique. Although his limited capacities may prevent him from reaching high levels of achievement, there is much that he can and needs to learn within his limits. But the teachers are sometimes operating rather in the dark, hoping that the recipe that has worked in the past with most children will work again. (Tansley and Gulliford, 1962).

Educationists as well as psychologists have conducted some experiments to devise special methods of teaching for slow learners. Their results (Curtis. K, and Shaver J.P., 1980; Gerald, 1977) indicate that the slow learners require short and simple methods of instruction based on concrete experiences. This will enable the slow learners to understand and use possible associations which will lengthen their retention and facilitate smooth recall.

One widely used means of adapting instruction to the needs of diverse students is called mastery learning (Block and Anderson, 1975; Block and Burns, 1976; Bloom, 1976). Mastery learning is a system of instruction that emphasises the achievement of instructional objectives by all students by allowing learning time to vary. The idea behind mastery learning is to make sure that all or almost all students have learned a particular skill to a pre-established level of Mastery before moving on to the next skill.

Mastery learning was first proposed as a solution to the problem of individual differences by Benjamin Bloom (1976). Bloom proposed that rather than providing all students with the same amount of instructional time and allowing learning to differ, perhaps we should require that all or almost all students reach a certain level of achievement by allowing time to differ. That is, Bloom suggests that we give students as much time and instruction as necessary to bring them all to a reasonable level of learning. This is exactly ensured in auto-instructional modules.

Bloom (1976) hypothesises that given additional instructional time, students who do not master their lessons in the time usually allowed should be able to reach achievement levels typically attained by only the most able students. In fact, he proposes that 80 per cent of all students should be able to achieve at a level usually attained by only 20 per cent of students, and that under these circumstances aptitude or ability should be nearly unrelated to achievement. Bloom argues that we should "treat" students until they reach a pre-established level of mastery. In the traditional instructional method, students start out with a certain distribution of skills. But, as instruction goes on, "the rich get richer and the poor get poorer"; that is, high achieving students gain more than low achievers. In contrast, when additional instruction is given to low achievers their performance comes to resemble that of the high achieving students.

The problem inherent in any mastery learning strategy is how to provide the additional instructional time to students who need it. In much of the research on mastery learning, this additional instruction is given outside of regular class time, such as after school or during recess. Those students who failed to meet a pre-established mastery criterion (such as 90 per cent correct on a quiz) following a lesson were given this extra corrective instruction until they could earn a 90 per cent score on a similar quiz. Research on mastery learning programmes that provide corrective instruction in addition to regular class time has generally found achievement gains, particularly for low achievers (Block and Burns, 1976; Bloom, 1976).

This mastery learning is the ultimate objective of multimedia modules which are auto instructional in nature and allow students to take as much time as they require for achieving mastery learning. Since these modules can be used in any setting convenient to the learner, the problem of providing additional instructional time can be easily overcome. Slow learning pace of the slow learners can be taken care of in this multimedia based modular approach, since they can learn the modules even outside the classroom setting at their own pace. So to provide appropriate level of instruction to the slow learners, the intervening instructional strategy can effectively make use of multimedia based modular approach.

Verbal instruction should be limited for the slow learners (Duncan. J., 1942 and Thomson *et al.*, 1947). They need maximum use of LTIM and HTIM for fast and perfect understanding. Project method and field trips are also essential to impart effective instruction. Direct experience and concrete examples are also of great help for the slow learners. Traditional lecture method does not take care of the above requirements.

It lays undue stress on verbal exposition and memorisation. What is wanted is mastery learning as well as application of knowledge and skill. This warrants a special intervening instructional strategy for the slow learners so that they can be enabled to cope with normal students. Multimedia based modular approach is such a strategy.

CONCEPT, MEANING, DEFINITION AND SIGNIFICANCE OF MULTIMEDIA

The present century is rightly called technological century due to the influence of advancements in the field of science and technology on the varied aspects of life, resulting in its modernisation. The impact of scientific and technological advancements on education is so great that it has given rise to a new discipline called Educational Technology.

To-day's classroom practices are quite different from those of yesterday. Similarly, the classroom practices in the coming century may be quite different from those of today. One can easily find out the explanation for these differences in the obvious impact of technological innovations and inventions. The shape of future school, colleges and universities is bound to change radically due to technological impact in the years to come. There is a greater need to gear education and teacher education to meet the future requirements of the society utilising the technological devices and chances. Educational technology has revolutionised the educational system. It has come in to stay for ever for the enrichment of educational and instructional processes. It has greatly influenced the teaching learning process.

The major problem of teaching in our schools is how to accommodate instruction to individual differences of the learners. Educational technology has developed new innovative practices and strategies for this purpose. One such strategy is multimedia based modular approach.

Readers Digest defines multimedia as combination of modes of communication, such as video, audio and text. According to Encyclopaedia of Education, the term "multimedia instructional system" refers to the use of appropriate and carefully selected varieties of learning experiences which, when presented to learner through selected teaching strategies, will reinforce and strengthen one another so that the learner will achieve predetermined and desired behavioural objectives.

. Multimedia means making appeal to different senses instead of one as in the traditional method. Multimedia includes High Technology Instructional Media (HTIM) and Low Technology Instructional Media ('LTIM) (G.S. Pillai, 1988).

In teaching learning process in classroom situation different media are used viz., video, computer, teaching machine, films, filmstrips and other projected and non projected aids to make learning more effective. This not only makes communication effective and impressive, but also helps in motivating the children and creating interest in the lessons. It also helps in understanding unfamiliar situations and aids in building concepts and development of creative thinking. Besides, it ignites the spark of curiosity.

Further, use of multimedia facilitates in overcoming certain inadequacies and deficiencies of the school system. The audio visual aids make the learning more effective particularly the individual and group learning. Under teacher student interaction it provides opportunities for teachers and students to work together in small groups to discuss, to question, to report, to be evaluated or to engage in other forms of personalised interaction outside the classroom experience. Thus, the multimedia can effectively bring forth better progress and developments in educational system.

The traditional teacher depends on verbal exposition. Considerable visualisation of objects and process is essential for formulation of accurate concepts among the students. A teacher using multimedia can make even difficult concept clear to a below average student easily.

Moreover, in this fast developing world, where knowledge explosion is taking place in every sphere, it is unreasonable to expect that the spoken or written words alone could convey the volume of relevant information to the learner. The role played by multimedia packages for educational purposes is highly significant. It helps to overcome barriers. It goes beyond the four walls of the classroom. It fulfils the gap in learning. Difficult processes can be shown with ease. Inaccessible places can be viewed by sitting in the cosy classroom.

Those who have properly implemented the multimedia instructional system have reported that outcomes exceeded both single medium channel utilisation and traditional verbal instruction (Georgiady *et al.*, 1967).

Multimedia devices are more capable of penetrating deeply into human character with an immediate excitement than any other single medium. When these multimedia packages are used as an integral part of the modules, the blend and the reinforcement of both will ensure effective learning.

Any discussion on multimedia without highlighting the current use of computers will be incomplete. One means of individualising instruction that has been receiving a great deal of attention in recent years is computer-assisted instruction or CAI. The decreasing cost and increasing availability of micro computers in schools have led researchers as well as teachers to become more interested in CAI (Becker, 1986).

The idea behind computer assisted instruction is to use the computer as a tutor to present information, give students practice, assess their level of understanding, and provide additional instruction, if needed. In theory, a well designed CAI programme is nearly perfect at providing appropriate levels of instruction, as it can analyse student responses immediately to determine whether to spend more time on a particular topic or skill. The computer can be quite effective in presenting ideas, using pictures or diagrams to reinforce concepts. Finally, for most students, the computer seems to have a motivating quality of its own, so that they work longer and harder when using it than they would on comparable paper-and-pencil tasks.

Computer assisted instruction has its roots in programmed instruction and in the behavioural theories of learning (Slavin, 1986). According to these theories, learning is accelerated by the use of controlled presentation of stimuli, followed by reinforcement based upon the learners responses. CAI Programmes stress drill practice exercises; others teach students facts and concepts. Whatever their differences, CAI Programmes generally share the following characteristics:

(i) Use of structured curriculum.

(ii) Letting students work at their pace.

(iii) Giving students controlled, frequent feed back and reinforcement and

(iv) Measuring performance quickly and giving students information on their performance.

Since most of the salient features of modularisation are incorporated in CAI programme, a CAI software developed as an integral part of multimedia based modules will, no doubt, facilitate the auto learning of slow learners.

MODULES—MEANING AND DEFINITION

Module is a self contained, suitably tested, auto instructional material. Modular approach provides a strategy for the teacher and the learner to mutually share the responsibility for learning. The teacher becomes a facilitator of learning, rather than the traditional way. A module is a self-contained and self-instructional material. It is self contained in the sense that everything is self-explanatory. It is a self-instructional package because each module has a set of objectives and it fulfils in developing the expected skills in the learner. Since it is an individualised instructional material, the learner can take his own time to complete the material. It is not time but achievement that is the criterion in a module.

A module will help the learners in the following ways:

(i) It develops learning autonomy in a learner because it is an auto learning material.

(ii) It ensures achievement of an expected standard.

(iii) It provides remedial instruction. The embedded tests and objective by objective movements help the learner to classify things.

Learning packages, Unipacs, learning activity packages, etc. are some of the titles used for a strategy useful for self-learning. But, as no title has gained universal acceptance as the phrase learning module; it is considered the general name for the strategy. Although, learning modules will differ, each can be expected to have similar elements and the sequence in the module.

Elements of Modules

A learning module should have the following elements:

(i) A title or topic designation

(ii) A list of major concepts to be learnt

(iii) The rationale for studying the module

(iv) A pre-assessment activity

(v) Objectives stated in behavioural terms

(vi) Guidelines for learner, teacher preparation

(vii) A detailed learning sequence

(viii) Summary

(ix) Suggested depth or quest activities

(x) A post assessment activity.

In order to maximise learning, suitable instructional materials in the form of modules may be developed. These modules should be validated before use. Self instructional modules are extensively used in different situations for efficient learning.

Components of an Instructional Module

(i) Entry test

(ii) Pre-test

(iii) Objectives

(iv) Introduction

(v) Development of learning material for objective I.

(vi) Diagrams, Sketches, pictures, examples, work sheets, embedded test, etc.

(vi) Development of learning material for objective II.

(vii) Diagrams, Sketches, pictures, examples, work sheets, drawings, embedded test, etc.,

(viii) Summary/Conclusion

(ix) Case study

(x) Post-test

(xi) Key to questions

(xii) References

(xiii) Projects/Guidelines for further action.

Special Features

The following are the special features of a module:

(i) Validated/tested material

(ii) Mass produced for use in institutions/for learning different subjects.

(iii) Participation of learner explicit

(iv) Specially suited for individual's self-learning.

Development of a Module

The first page depicts the main unit and the single conceptual sub unit covered in the module. Also, it reflects the components of the learning modules, *i.e.*, development or construction pattern of the module. The next page gives necessary instruction as to how to use the module. Instruction is followed by an entry test which consists of objective type items on the preliminary knowledge required for learning the module. If a student fails to attain minimum level achievement, he may not understand the module and so he should not go through the learning module unless his entering behaviour is strengthened. The pre-test follows the entry test. The pretest is also an objective type test, which helps to self evaluate the student's status when he proceeds with the module. It is followed by introduction of the topic. General objectives and specific objectives are listed out. Then the relevant learning materials will be presented for the objectives stated. Necessary diagrams, sketches, pictures, worksheets, examples, dimensional drawings, summary and conclusion, case study, etc. will be included in the material suitably. Immediately after the presentation of the subject for each objective, it will be suitably recapitulated. Provision is made for formative evaluation in the course of the module in the form of embedded tests. After all the learning materials are presented, a post-test is given. This post-test is also of objective type but the items are different from that of the pre-test. Necessary bibliographical references, assignments and guidelines for further follow-up action should find a place in the module.

Once the learning material under the identified topic is drafted, incorporating the components of a module is the next step. After that, it requires editing, reviewing and validating. Editing has to be done with reference to accuracy and relevance of the material, style, vocabulary, density of presenting the facts and content interest. Only editing can unearth many inadequacies prior testing. Once the editing is over, the material is ready for try-outs. Try-out helps in refining the module and makes it relevant to the target population. For a module, the try-out may be conducted in two ways:

(i) Individual try-out

(ii) Group try-out.

Individual Try-out

Under the individual try-out, the module developer sits face to face with the randomly selected individuals of the target students one at a time. This gives an opportunity to the developer to study the reaction of the learner in respect to the materials presented. The number of individuals to be tried out depends upon the quality of the draft of the material and the degree of refinement required. The developer notes down the time taken for reading and understanding. Clarifications asked, remarks made and the scores obtained in the pre-test and post-test etc., should be noted down. On the basis of these ratings and analysis of the tryout, the developer makes correction, modifications, refinement etc. then and there. Then, after completion of a number of individual try-outs, the material becomes better refined.

Group Try-out

Under group try-out, the cyclostyled copies of developed modules are administered to a group of students of the same target population. Separate answer sheets may be provided for writing the answers to the pre-test and post-test items. The creation of congenial atmosphere and establishment of proper rapport are the vital requirements for group try-out. The students must be instructed about the nature of this auto instructional material and what is expected of them along with the purpose of the try-out. The reaction of the students during the try-out should be noted down, so that they may be considered for further refinement. Evaluation of the answer sheet will bring to light the per centage of incorrect responses and their level of mastery achievement. Based on the scores, norms may be evolved. The post-test score minus the pre-test score will be the gain score which can be attributed to the effectiveness of the modules.

Appraisal of the Module

In general, learning modules need to be subjected to critical appraisal of structure and content. Critical appraisals need to be done in the following seven areas:

(i) Objectives

(ii) Subject matter

(iii) Design characteristics

(iv) Learning activities

(v) Adaptability

(vi) Validity, and

(vii) Evaluation

On completion of all these processes, the learning module can be presented to individual students.

IMPORTANCE OF MULTIMEDIA BASED MODULES

Multimedia based module is the latest trend now advocated in learning. Modules are prepared on the same topic under different media softwares to suit the different tastes and interests of the students according to the facilities available. The components of a multimedia based module include modular lecture unit, group discussion unit, role-play unit, workshop unit, individual study unit, film unit, audio tape unit, etc. Here the same components of a module as discussed will be incorporated but the nature of the medium will be dominating in the presentation of the particular module.

When different varieties of modules are kept in the library, the interested students can use one or more variety for learning the topic. While one may like to listen to an audio lecture on the topic, another may like to see a video on it. The multimedia based modules in this way suit to the interests of different individuals. Since these modules motivate the slow learners to a very great extent, they promote their achievement ultimately. These modules can be used by the teachers of different classes also. They will remain as an asset to the institutions. The slow learners can take them home and learn them at their own pace.

NEED FOR MULTIMEDIA BASED MODULES IN TEACHING SLOW LEARNERS

Slow learners constitute such a significant per centage of school population that they cannot be ignored. Children of today are the future citizens and they are going to be the pillars of the country. Hence, it is essential to ensure that each pillar is as strong as the other. This envisages a special instructional strategy for the slow learners.

Multimedia based modules enable the slow learners to develop their skill of learning and to cope with normal students. Slow learners have limited span of attention and poor retention. They lack proper concentration also. So any conventional method of classroom instruction is found inadequate for them. This necessitates developing multimedia based modules so that they can cope with normal students.

It is clear from different studies made in this regard that when the learning materials are presented through concrete situations, the slow learners', concentration and attention do not differ significantly from that of a normal child. Since multimedia based modules ensure concrete presentation of instructional materials, the slow learners can surmount the problem of abstract thinking.

The slow learners evince keen interest in learning where the relationships are clearly demonstrated. This type of demonstration ignites the spark of rational thinking in the minds of the slow learners. A multimedia based module serves this purpose.

As the slow learners have poor retention power, they require more practice and revicion when compared with normal students. A multimedia based module provides ample opportunity for all these aspects. Multimedia based module takes care of the short span of attention of slow learners. Further, the module takes care of the following vital remedial programmes:

(i) Grading of teaching materials taking into consideration the capacity and requirement of children.

(ii) Short frequent lessons instead of the long lessons.

(iii) Giving importance to practice, drill, review, repetition and direction.

Since multimedia based modules are self-contained and self-instructional, the slow learners are bound to learn at their own pace with minimum or no inhibition. The objective stated in the beginning, the sequence of learning materials presented in the body and the evaluation procedure at the end will take care of repetition, direction, drill and review.

Moreover, multimedia based modules facilitate concrete presentation, clear demonstration and better perceptual grasp. A close study of VIII standard syllabi shows that a resourceful teacher can prepare modules and the required multimedia aids making use of the resources locally available. A little pain taken by the teacher will ensure optimal gain for the slow learners.

Multimedia based modules bear the following advantages from the slow learners' point of view:

(i) The learners are involved in the learning process and their commitment to the task is increased.

(ii) A large part of the modules will create interest among students as it is a novel experiment.

(iii) The students have the full control over the rate of study. So they can progress at their own pace.

(iv) The consequences of failures are reduced. Each student can master each module completely before proceeding to the next.

(v) Each student can participate in the decision whether he has learned the subject matter adequately.

(vi) It may be practical for some modules to be checked out as study at home resulting in saving of time.

(vii) Each student can develop a sense of responsibility for his own learning.

All these factors emphasise that there is a growing need for multimedia based modules for mastery level learning and the need is, in fact, greater when the slow learner is involved in the learning process. The present study is an earnest attempt, in this regard, to develop and to measure the effectiveness of multimedia based modular approach in teaching of slow learners.

The review of related literature is presented in the succeeding chapter.

2

REVIEW OF RELATED LITERATURE

INTRODUCTION

Good, Barr and Scates (1935) state that as the competent physician must keep abreast of the latest discoveries in the field of medicine, the research worker and investigator should become familiar with the location and sources of educational information. Study of related literatures implies locating, reading and evaluating reports of researches as well as reports of casual observations and opinions that are related to the investigator's planned research project.

Related literature includes theoretic discussions, reviews of the status of knowledge by authorities, philosophical papers, description and evaluation of current practices and empirical researches. Review of related researches is indispensable to get a clear cut perspective of the problem.

In the words of Walter R. Borg (1965) the literature in any field forms the foundation upon which all future work will be built. Scanning of relevant research reports guides the researcher in the right direction, highlighting the pit falls of the earlier studies showing him the landmarks achieved. Also, a synthesised collection of previous studies helps the researcher to identify the significant overlaps and gaps among the prior ones. The investigator can probe into the neglected areas which need more concentration. Further, the review of related research enables the investigator to get to the frontier in the field of his problem. Until the investigator has learnt what others have done and what still remains to be done in his area, he can not develop a research project that will contribute to furthering knowledge in his field. It makes the researcher aware of the research possibilities that have been overlooked. His focus on these areas may pave the way to break new grounds and come out successful with new theories and principles which may be of permanent value in the field of teaching and learning.

The literature so far available shows that a good number of studies have been conducted on the use of multimedia in formal and non-formal education in India and abroad. Many are the studies made on the effectiveness of video instruction in teaching process. Quite a few studies have been conducted to prove and measure the effectiveness of modular approach. Regarding low achievement and slow learning also decisive studies have been conducted both in India and abroad. These studies are elaborative analytical besides being exhaustive. In this chapter an attempt is made to present a summary of literature related to the research topic under two broad categories such as studies conducted in India and the studies done abroad.

STUDIES CONDUCTED IN INDIA

Studies Conducted on Multimedia in Formal Education in India

Various studies on multimedia have been conducted in India. It ranges from studies on audio-visual aids to studies on computer application. These studies are presented under two classifications such as studies conducted on multimedia in formal education and studies conducted on multimedia in non-formal education.

Ahuja and Ahuja (1985) conducted a study on "demonstration of audio-visual and reading aids to school students and their reading speed in three languages—Kannada, Hindi and English".

One of the main objectives of the study was the general evaluation of the audio-visual aids.

The major findings of the study were:

(i) The closed circuit programme was liked by the students and was found to be very effective both from the language and comprehension point of view by more than 95 per cent of the students.

(ii) The students were not much benefitted by the three films on reading purchased from an outside source.

(iii) More than 95 per cent of the students found the film produced by CILL, Mysore very interesting and clear and could fully follow the message of the film.

Antonisamy (1989) studied the effectiveness of teaching environmental concepts to school drop-outs through video and charts.

The main objectives of the study were:

(1) To prepare a video programme on various environmental concepts for school drop-outs.

(2) To prepare charts on various environmental concepts for school drop-outs.

(3) To study the effectiveness of teaching environmental concepts through video and charts. The main findings of the study were as follows:

   (i) Teaching the environmental concepts to the drop-outs through video was more effective than teaching the environmental concepts through charts.

   (ii) Teaching the environmental concepts to the drop-outs through video was found to be effective.

   (iii) Teaching the environmental concepts to the drop-outs through charts was also found to be effective.

   (iv) There was no difference between boys and girls, in understanding the environmental concepts taught through the video programme.

   (v) Teaching the environmental concepts to boys and girls through video was found to be effective.

(vi) Teaching the environmental concepts to boys and girls through charts was found to be effective.

Anupama Shah and Sushmita Mandal (1993) made a study on 'effectiveness of three instructional strategies for higher education'. Lecture cum live demonstration, video film and booklet were the strategies followed. They found that video film was the best strategy followed by lecture cum demonstration and booklet methods. They suggested that video technology should be made more available to the educational institutions.

N. Balasubramanian and M. Yoganandam (1994) made "a comparative study for effectiveness in improving English pronunciation - trained teacher Vs technology" with the following objectives.

(i) To develop an audio package for improving the pronunciation of English vowels, diphthongs and consonants among std V pupils.

(ii) To find out the relative effectiveness of the developed audio packages over direct teaching by trained teacher in the production of correct English sound by Std V pupils.

The study concluded that though the training given by the trained teacher and that given through pre-recorded audio cassette are almost similar in their effectiveness in improving the pronunciation of English sounds among std V pupils, both the trainings fail to improve one or the other aspect of English sounds. While the training given by the teacher fails to improve the pronunciation of diphthongs, the training given through the pre-recorded audio cassette fails to improve that of vowels among std V pupils. Hence, it is concluded that the teacher and the technology should be complementary to each other in any scheme of education. Technology can be used effectively as an aid in the classroom and teacher's involvement in it will make the teaching learning process more effective.

Basu (1981) studied "effectiveness of multimedia programmed materials in teaching physics". The main objectives of the study were:

(i) To prepare different types of programmed learning materials, semi-programme, linear programme, branching programme, hybrid programme and compare their effectiveness in classroom instruction.

(ii) To compare the relative effectiveness of different instructional strategies employing multimedia programmed class teaching on the criteria of immediate achievement, retention and delayed retention.

The study arrived at the following conclusions:

(i) There are significant differences among the means of different strategies, on the overall achievement. Multimedia semi-programmed instruction was better than the strategy of the multimedia linear programmed instruction and the multimedia hybrid programmed instruction was better than multimedia branching programmed instruction.

(ii) Multimedia programmed instruction enabled the learners to reach mastery level. The scores were between 80-86 out of 100.

(iii) There was significant difference in the achievement through different strategies due to difference in ability.

Bhatt (1992) conducted a study on "effectiveness of three modes of teaching science on students' achievement". The following were the objectives of the investigation:

(i) To develop video cassettes of TV lessons covering ten lessons of selected topics in standard X science.

(ii) To teach the students in three groups (boys and girls each) through the following modes:

(a) TV lessons with guidance notes;

(b) Experiments, charts and demonstration; and

(c) Lecture-cum-discussion.

(iii) To compare the results of learning in different ways *i.e.*, to find out the

(a) Comparative effects of learning through three different modes;

(b) Comparison of results of two sex groups; and

(c) Intersection comparison of results of three sections, viz., physics, chemistry and biology.

From the results of the study, the major findings are given as follows:

(i) TV lessons were significantly more effective than lesson through experiment-cum-demonstration and lecture-cum-discussion.

(ii) TV lessons were found quite feasible and useful for secondary school students, in science education; their usefulness would increase if they are prepared with utmost care.

(iii) As regards to the different sex, no clear-cut evidence of difference in performance was found.

(iv) The significance of differences between different sections of science, *i.e.*, Physics, Chemistry and Biology reveal that there was not a single evidence of significance of difference between Physics and Biology. In few cases the significance of difference between Physics and Chemistry as well as Chemistry and Biology was seen.

(v) Opinions regarding the TV lessons indicated that they were found quite interesting to the participants, and they warmly welcomed learning through this type of lessons.

(vi) The order of the methods, in view of preference and as assigned by the participants, was found as under:

(a) TV lesson

(b) Experiment-cum-demonstration method, and

(c) Lecture-cum-discussion method.

Desai (1985) conducted "an investigation into the efficiency of different instructional media in the teaching of science to the pupils of class VIII in relation to certain variables".

The major objective of the study was to compare the achievement of pupils in science learning through different instructional media and the traditional way of teaching. The major findings were:

(i) Programmed learning approach was more effective than the traditional way of teaching science.

(ii) Studies with discussion approach was more effective than traditional approach.

(iii) The experimental approach was more effective than traditional way of teaching science.

(iv) In teaching science, the experimental approach was the most effective of all the approaches.

Edward Sahayaraj, S. (1994) conducted an experimental study on "effectiveness of lecture method supplemented with low-cost teaching aids in learning physics by the higher secondary plus one students" with the following objectives.

(i) To prepare low cost teaching aids to teach physics to higher secondary students.

(ii) To find out whether the higher secondary +1 students improved their achievement in physics after teaching physics by lecture method supplemented with low-cost teaching aids.

(iii) To find out whether there exists any significant difference between the post-test scores of average students in control group and experimental group.

(iv) To find out whether there exists any significant difference between the post-test scores of the below average students in the control group and experimental group.

After analysis, the study arrived at the following conclusions:

(i) Low-cost teaching aids could be prepared for most of the units in physics.

(ii) The Hr. Sec. +1 students in experimental group significantly improved their achievement in physics after teaching physics by lecture method supplemented with low-cost teaching aids.

(iii) There is significant difference between the post-test scores of average students in control group taught through traditional lecture method and experimental group after teaching physics by lecture method supplemented with low-cost teaching aids. The performance of experimental group average students is better than the performance of control group average students.

(iv) There is significant difference between the post-test scores of the below average students taught through traditional lecture method and the below average students of experimental group taught by lecture method supplemented with low-cost teaching aids. The performance of experimental group below average students is better than the performance of control group below average students.

A study by George (1966) entitled, "an enquiry into the scope and effectiveness of audio-visual instruction in improving English teaching in Kerala State in the first three years of school course", concluded the following;

(i) Teacher did not use audio-visual aids because of heavy cost, heavy syllabus, insufficient number of material aids and lack of skill and special training.

(ii) Pupils taught by using audio-visual aids achieved higher than those taught by the usual method and the use of audio-visual aids did not require more time when compared to ordinary teaching

Golani (1982) studied, "the use of audio-visual aids in the secondary schools of the District Thane". The objectives of the study were:

(i) To create awareness amongst teachers and school heads about the importance of audio-visual aids.

(ii) To help raise the academic standard of secondary schools of Thane District.

(iii) To know the existing situation regarding audio-visual material in the secondary schools.

(iv) To elicit the opinions of headmasters and teachers about the measures for providing better and improvised material for audio-visual education.

The main findings of the study were:

(i) According to the opinions of the secondary school teachers teaching aids were essential and useful in developing clear concepts and stimulating learning.

(ii) Audio-visual aids were expensive and some schools could not afford for them.

(iii) The audio-visual aids were not available in rural areas due to transport difficulties.

(iv) Teachers lacked time to prepare the aids.

(v) No incentive is given to teachers for using teaching aids.

(vi) Good use of aids could be realized if only teachers were thoroughly trained.

A study was conducted by Hianman and Purushothaman (1988) about "the instruction through interactive video in developing the skills viz.:

(a) keen observation,

(b) identification of a problem,

(c) inference drawing,

(d) formulating hypotheses,

(e) divergent thinking, and

(f) generalisation.

The analysis of the data revealed that experimental group pupils developed the above mentioned skills, better than control group pupils. The more interesting part of the study is that there were very interesting correlations within the skills chosen for development in the experimental group. This paper further suggests suitable strategies for instruction through interactive video.

Idayavani (1991) conducted a study on "developing a video programme on weathering and work of the rivers in physical geography for higher secondary students". The main objectives of the study were:

(i) To prepare a video programme on weathering and work of the rivers for instructional use of higher secondary students of the second year.

(ii) To find out whether—the students improve their achievement after viewing the video programme on weathering and work of the rivers.

(iii) To find out whether the male and female students improve their achievement after viewing the video programme on weathering and work of the rivers.

The main findings of the study were:

(i) The students improved their learning of the concepts of weathering and work of the rivers after viewing video programme.

(ii) The male and female students taught by video method are equal in their learning the concepts of weathering and work of river.

(iii) The students taught by video method performed better than the students taught by traditional lecture method in the learning of the concepts of weathering and work of the rivers.

Jayalakshmi (1992) developed a video programme and measured its effectiveness in teaching balanced diet to higher secondary home science students and community people. The objectives of the study are as follows:

(i) To develop a video programme on teaching of balanced diet to higher secondary home science students and community people.

(ii) To find out whether the higher secondary home science students improve their achievement after teaching balanced diet by lecture method.

(iii) To find out whether the higher secondary home science students improve their achievement after viewing the video programme on balanced diet.

(iv) To find out whether the community people improve their knowledge after teaching balanced diet by lecture method.

(v) To find out whether the community people improve their knowledge after viewing the video programme on balanced diet.

(vi) To find out whether there exists any difference in learning of balanced diet between higher secondary home science students and community people taught through lecture method and video method.

The study arrived at the following conclusions:

(i) The higher secondary home science students significantly improved their learning of balanced diet after teaching through traditional lecture method.

(ii) The higher secondary home science students significantly improved their learning of balanced diet after teaching through video method.

(iii) The community people significantly improved their learning of balanced diet after teaching through traditional lecture method.

(iv) The community people significantly improved their learning of balanced diet after teaching through video method.

(v) There is significant difference in the learning of balanced diet between higher secondary home science students taught through traditional method and video method. The achievement of the students in balanced diet is higher in video method than in traditional lecture method.

(vi) There is significant difference in the learning of balanced diet between community people taught through traditional lecture method and video method. The achievement of the community people in balanced diet is higher in video method than in traditional lecture method.

Kalimuthu's (1991) study on "developing a video programme on environmental pollution in biology for higher secondary students" reveals the following findings:

(i) Both the male and female students improved their learning of the concepts of environmental pollution after viewing the video programme.

(ii) Both the male and female students learned more concepts of environmental pollution when they were taught by video method than by traditional lecture method.

An experimental study was conducted by Kumar (1981) to know the "relative effectiveness of three methods of instruction-exposition method, programmed learning method and multimedia method in science education".

The results of the study gave the following findings:

(i) The multimedia method was more effective than the expository method.

(ii) Programmed learning method was more effective than the expository method.

(iii) Retention in learning by multimedia method was higher than by the other two methods.

(iv) Retention in learning by the programmed learning group and the expository group was equal.

(v) There was no interaction between the three methods of instruction and the level of intelligence.

A study was conducted by Kumar (1981) about the "effectiveness of self-instructional audio-cassettes in developing teaching skills among students" with the following objectives:

(i) To develop instructional materials for the skills of questioning, explaining and illustrating with examples.

(ii) To prepare audio cassettes of the instructional materials for the above mentioned teaching skills.

(iii) To develop the above mentioned skills with examples through self-instructional audio cassettes.

(iv) To examine the effect of such audio cassettes on the general teaching competence of student teachers.

The main findings of the study were:

(i) The experimental groups exposed to both the treatments did better performance than control group.

(ii) The self instructional audio-cassettes were effective for developing different teaching skills.

(iii) Immediate feed back through audio-cassettes was an effective way of improving the performance of student teachers in the use of different skills.

An investigation was made by Madhur Gupta (1989) on the topic' "two strategies of computer assisted instruction in chemistry". The main objectives of the study were:

(i) To design two strategies of computer-assisted instruction.

(ii) To study the relative effectiveness of two strategies of CAI in chemistry.

(iii) To compare the mean retention scores of two strategies of CAI in chemistry.

The study concluded that the students under first strategy scored significantly higher than the students under strategy II in terms of their mean gain scores and mean retention scores in the criterion test.

P. Mallick and P.K. Sahoo (1994) conducted an experimental study on "effectiveness of school level E.T.V. programme with and without talk back facilities in terms of achievement of rural background students" with the following objectives:

(i) To study the level of achievement of students on E.T.V. lessons.

(ii) To study the achievement of students on topics telecast with talk back and without talkback.

The study concluded that ETV programmes with or without talkback were effective. With regard to only one programme interaction facility through talkback followed by TV show was found more effective than TV viewing without talkback. It may be due to the reasons that the TV programmes were presented in so impressive forms that further interaction between students and teachers did not bring additional effect at significant level. Of course, the post-test scores show that in the case of all the lessons ETV + Talkback group had slightly higher achievement than the ETV without talkback group students.

Maria Araselvi (1996) conducted an experimental study to measure the "effectiveness of educational audio and video cassettes in teaching mathematics". After analysis, the study gave the following conclusions:

(i) Both the strategies *i.e.,* audio instruction and video instruction were more effective than the traditional lecture method.

(ii) The video instruction was more effective than audio instruction in teaching mathematics to the students of class VIII.

(iii) The relative effectiveness of audio and video cassettes differed from group to group. They were more effective to below average students, moderately effective to average students. As for above average students, the effectiveness was not significant, since they could make a similar rate of progress only as the control group students taught through traditional lecture method.

Oberai (1981) studied the "development of radio-vision as an instructional system" with the following objectives:

(i) To compare the radio-vision method of instruction in terms of academic gains on the part of the subjects.

(ii) To compare radio-vision as a medium of instruction to other classroom methods in terms of academic gain on the part of the students.

The major findings of the investigator were:

(i) The radio-vision group obtained significantly higher mean scores on the recognition test than the conventional lecture group.

(ii) All the radio-vision groups except black and white radio-vision group obtained significantly higher mean scores than the group receiving instruction through the traditional method in the final experiment.

(iii) Group of colour radio-vision plus work book obtained significantly higher mean score in the recall test than the other group.

Phutela (1980) studied "utilisation and comprehensibility of school television programmes in Delhi Centre for Educational Technology (NCERT)".

The major finding of the investigation was, the results of the four out of the five comprehensive tests showed real difference in the learning of subject matter, indicating that the lessons were well understood.

Ramachandra (1992) studied the use of visual aids by teachers of University of Agricultural Sciences, Bangalore.

The major objectives of the study were:

(i) To evaluate the current use of audio-visual aids by teachers of Agricultural University.

(ii) To identify factors governing the use of visual aids.

(iii) To find out association between visual aids use level and factors governing their use.

(iv) To find out the association between the visual aids use level and the visual aids determinant.

(v) To identify the overall influence of factors determining visual aids use level of teachers.

The study revealed the following:

(i) Visual aids use level index was low in basic sciences and humanities when compared to agricultural colleges, veterinary colleges and fishery colleges.

(ii) The association between the age of teachers and visual aids use level was not significant.

(iii) The association between visual aids use indices and teachers qualifications, training, status was significant.

(iv) Other factors *i.e.*, number of times the course was offered, and number of students per class did not have significant association with the visual aids use level.

(v) The association between the visual aids use level and the visual aids determinant was positive and significant.

Ramar (1994) undertook an experimental study on "effectiveness of multimedia based modular approach with special reference to low achievers" with the following objectives:

(i) To develop multimedia based modules for all the subjects of Std VIII.

(ii) To assess whether there is any significant difference between the pre-test and post-test mean scores of experimental group slow learners.

(iii) To know whether there exists any significant difference between the post-test scores of control group low achievers and experimental group low achievers.

(iv) To know whether there is any significant difference between the post-test scores of experimental group low achievers and the normal group students.

After analysis, the study arrived at the following conclusions:

(i) Multimedia based modules can be developed to teach all the subjects of Std VIII.

(ii) There is significant difference between the pre-test and the post-test mean scores of experimental group low achievers. Their achievement in the post-test is higher than their achievement in the pre-test. This tremendous progress in the post-test performance can be attributed to the effectiveness of multimedia based modular approach.

(iii) There is significant difference between the post-test mean scores of control group low achievers and experimental group low achievers. Though, they were alike in the pre-test performance, the experimental group low achievers showed a significantly higher achievement than the control group low achievers in the post-test. This rate of progress is the resultant product of implementation of multimedia based modular approach.

(iv) There is significant difference between the post-test mean scores of experimental group low achievers and normal group students. The achievement of normal group students is higher than the achievement of experimental group low achievers. However, the experimental group low achievers could narrow down the gap between them and the normal group students in the post-test. The narrowed down gulf of difference between the experimental group low achievers and the normal students bears testimony to the effectiveness of multimedia based modular approach.

A study done by Ramendra Dasgupta (1969), aimed at comparing the PSI with conventional method (lecture discussion) for technological curriculum on a more rigorous basis and collecting of detailed feed back from the technology students.

The results of the study show that the performance of the PSI sample had been significantly better than that of the conventional sample.

Sastry (1982) used toys/models and figures to teach children. The children who were taught using models, toys and figures had better achievement in the post-test than those taught without the above visual facilities. Toys, models and figures are therefore, effective instructional media when compared to conventional lecture method.

Selvaraj. M (1992) studied the "role of mass-media in creating population awareness among rural people in Sakkottai Block" with the following objectives:

(i) To find out the role of mass-media in creating population awareness among rural people.

(ii) To find out the role of TV, radio, cinema and print media in creating population awareness among rural people.

(iii) To study whether people differ in their perception with regard to the role of mass media in creating population awareness in terms of certain biographical variables.

After analysis, the study gave the following conclusions.

The rural people estimate the positive role of mass media in creating population awareness among people. They consider that TV, radio and print media have been playing a significant role in creating awareness among the people with regard to ill effects of population on social, economic, political, cultural and educational spheres of human life. But to them, motion pictures are not involved in this process to a great extent. The people maintain that TV, radio and the press highlight the consequences of over population such as unemployment problem, environmental degradation, poverty and economic backwardness etc.

TV, radio, cinema and press play a significant role in creating awareness related to family planning. The films also play a role in this regard. The mass-media have been playing a positive role in creating awareness in small family norms, birth control methods and contraceptives. In general, mass media play a positive role in giving knowledge about population except motion picture.

Sethi (1976) Studied a programme in English spelling in relation to visual and auditory presentation with the following objectives:

(i) To find out the relative merits of visual and auditory models of presentation for learning programmed materials.

(ii) To find the comparative effects of visual and auditory models of programmed materials between boys and girls.

The study arrived at the following conclusions:

(i) Auditory mode was found superior to visual mode.

(ii) Girls performed better than boys.

(iii) There was significant relation between auditory and sex interaction, Auditory and time factors were not found significant.

(iv) Boys seemed to perform better on delayed tests.

Sinnathambi (1991) conducted a study on "developing a video programme on energetics in chemistry for higher secondary students". The main objectives of the study were:

(i) To prepare a video programme on energy for instructional use of the higher secondary students of second year.

(ii) To find out whether the students improve their achievement after viewing the video programme on energy.

The study reveals the following:

(i) The students improved their learning of concepts on energy after viewing the video programme.

(ii) The students taught by video method learned more concepts on energy than the students taught by traditional classroom method.

Subramanian (1982) studied "the effectiveness of two different methods of teaching reading in primary schools". Standard III with 81 pupils, was divided into three groups. Each group was given different instructional treatment:

(a) Flash cards

(b) Collateral reading

(c) Control group

The results show that the group subjected to flash cards performed better than the other two groups. It is, therefore, concluded that flash cards are more effective than collateral reading method at primary school level.

Sumita Ray and Poonamkumari (1991) studied the 'effectiveness of design elements of flash cards for nutrition education'.

The findings of the study were:

(i) The effectiveness of the design was determined through first ranked design elements, mean scores obtained from two sets of rates for short and distance viewing, and the combined mean scores along with coefficient of variations. The findings revealed that the per centage of rates assigning first rank to design elements ranged from 63.30 to 81.60.

Vibha Joshi (1992) conducted a study on "effectiveness of school television programmes in science" with the following objectives:

(1) To study the STV programmes in science at the secondary school level in terms of:

   (i) Instructional objectives

   (ii) Number of programmes telecast

   (iii) Content—coverage, adequacy and accuracy

   (iv) The extent to which media attributes and limitations of television are being taken care of.

   (v) Suitability of the organisation of learning experiences.

   (vi) Resources involved in production and related problems.

(2) To study the impact of STV programmes in science at the secondary school level on the students' performance in terms of:

   (i) Scholastic achievement (as related to the exposed topics)

   (ii) Scientific attitude.

The findings of the study are given as under:

(i) The frequency of the STV programmes was insufficient.

(ii) The content of the STV programmes was adequate as well as accurate.

(iii) For the selection of the topics for STV programmes, the attributes and limitations of the medium (television) were mostly considered but many a time they had been overlooked due to certain handicaps. The procedure employed for the selection of topics for STV programmes was found to be appropriate.

(iv) The allotment of topics was sometimes in accordance with the interest of the personnel but always in line with their capability and mostly in tune with feasibility.

- There was a committee for the allotment/distribution of topics in the TV branch.
- The time allotted for the preparation of STV programme was found to be insufficient most of the times.
- The time length and the duration of STV programmes were found satisfactory.
- The transmission of the STV programmes was found to be irregular.
- The presentation of the STV programmes was not satisfactory in terms of the reception and the quality of the presentation.
- The utilisation of the STV programmes was not satisfactory at all.
- The evaluation of the STV programmes was a routine exercise.

(v) There is a need for time to time orientation and rigorous training of the persons involved in the planning, production and utilisation of the STV programmes.

(vi) The TV branch and the STV unit in the TV centre are the two main bodies involved in STV programmes.

Critique of the Studies Under this Sub-head

It is very difficult to provide critique in respect of each study because these studies are usually referred to in journals or survey books, which provide us with only abstracts of the studies. However, an attempt is made subhead-wise to connect and contrast findings that are in some instances clearly contradictory.

Though, quite a number of studies have been conducted on multimedia in India, most of the studies are experimental studies intended to measure the effectiveness of certain medium or media on the achievement of students in specific subject(s).

Most of the studies have been made to measure the effectiveness of video instruction on achievement of students in specific subject(s) (Basu, 1981; Hianman and Purushothaman, 1988; Sinnathambi, 1991;). Some investigators have developed their own video packages and measured their effectiveness in teaching specific subject (Idaya Vani, 1991; Jayalakshmi, 1992; Kalimuthu, 1991; Sinnathambi, 1991). Though, all the above studies highlight the efficacy of video instruction, they are silent with regard to cost effectiveness and time effectiveness. Similarly, their affordability and feasibility in Indian school settings have not been clearly indicated. There are a few studies to assess the relative effectiveness of video instruction in comparison to other mode(s) of instruction (Desai, 1985; Kumar, 1981; Maria Araselvi, 1996;). In these studies also, overall achievement has been measured and there is no reference to relative cost and time effectiveness. How many schools will be able to afford for video and TV is a nagging question which remains still unanswered.

Many experimental studies have been carried out to measure ineffectiveness of school TV programmes (Mallick and Sahoo, 1994; Phutela, 1980; Vibha Joshi, 1993). Though, these studies establish the efficacy, they are critical about the suitability of some programmes and time allotment (Vibha Joshi, 1993). Only one survey study on mass media has been made which points out the relative strengths of TV, radio, cinema and print media in reaching out to the rural population. Adequate studies have been attempted to verify the efficacy of low cost teaching aids which are affordable and feasible in Indian school settings (Ahuja and Ahuja, 1985; Antonisamy, 1989; Edward Sahayaraj, 1994; Kumar, 1981; Ramachandra, 1992; Sastry, 1982; Subramanian, 1982). Though the solitary study on CAI of Madhur Gupta (1982) indicates efficacy, it is silent over its applicability in Indian school setting.

Studies Conducted on Multimedia in Non-Formal Education in India

Though not adequate, some studies on multimedia have been conducted in non-formal education in India. Such studies are presented under this subheading.

Baskar (1990) studied the 'effectiveness of teaching social concepts to the working children through video method'. The main objectives of the study were:

(i) To produce a video programme on social concepts for working children.

(ii) To study the effectiveness of teaching social concepts by video method.

(iii) To study the difference in learning of the social concepts between male and female children taught by video method.

(iv) To study the effectiveness of teaching social concepts by traditional lecture method.

(v) To study the difference in learning of social concepts between male and female children taught by traditional lecture method.

The main findings of the study were as follows:

(i) Teaching the social concepts to the working children through video was more effective than teaching by traditional lecture method.

(ii) The male children learned more social concepts than the female children when they were taught by video method.

(iii) There was no difference between male and female children in learning the social concepts when they were taught by traditional lecture method.

Bhangoo, S. and Kaur, S. (1989) studied the "effectiveness of educational video films in home science for rural women—an action experiment".

The study gave the following findings.

(i) Video film when used alone can be an effective method of teaching and that adult rural women gain a significant amount of knowledge by this method. It is specially recommended for such topic as the 'use of colour' which are difficult to create in the classroom situation and can be best presented through actual settings shown through film.

Cherian (1986) conducted "a study to analyse the selected health and hygiene, nutrition and family planning programmes by Television and its impacts on acquisition of knowledge by rural people of the selected village of Kheda District, Gujarat State, India".

The study showed that the women gained more knowledge than men by viewing the TV programme. TV viewing helped the women and men to gain significant amount of knowledge about green vegetables, polio vaccination and leproscopy.

According to Holtzman (1981) the results of numerous studies done in India to investigate the role of television in the learning process, point to the effective role of this medium in creating general awareness and increasing knowledge. Television as a medium cannot bring about behavioural change unless supported by a interpersonal face-to-face network. It can help to develop a positive attitude, it can open a window to the world. In this function of incidental learning, television success is influenced by a variety of factors including the role assigned to education by a society and the interrelationship between the educational and media systems.

Kannan (1976) used participatory research method to study the impact of farmer's programmes in TV on a village in Tamil Nadu. The findings of the study are as follows:

(i) Development in communication does not bring significant degree of success in places where there is a high rate of illiteracy.

(ii) If the programmes satisfy the local requirements of people, the communication process will prove a real success.

(iii) Communication must have clarity of purpose. At the same time, it must be simple for the common folk to understand.

Kaur and Koshy (1970) undertook a study to find out the "impact of television on farm women in Delhi". The study proved that the farm women gained significant amount of knowledge about the three selected practices shown on television. The mean per centage of retained knowledge varied from 72.38 per cent to 83.26 per cent when measured after 15 days of each telecast.

This clearly indicates that television as a medium of educational technology can be very effectively used in teaching women in nonformal setting.

According to Mody (1978) the important findings of social evaluation studies on SITE are as follows:

Socio-economic status was found to be inversely related to TV viewing as the small farmers and landless labourers formed the greater part of audience. TV viewing did not displace or increase the use of other media, but it did not increase contact with village level extension agent. There were statistically significant gains in knowledge of preventive health measures. Children exposed to TV in the classroom showed significant increase in their language development. The presence of TV in the school had no impact on enrolments and attendance, because of poor economic condition and need for children to help their parents in the household / farming activities. TV school teachers were excited about TV as a classroom aid, but they found 'enrichment' programme unrelated to their syllabus.

Mullick (1981) developed learning materials for non-formal education of girls in the age group of 11-14 years in rural area on health education. The study was divided into two phases. The first phase was study of effectiveness of tape-slide presentation for teaching illiterate children. The second phase was the study of attitude of teachers towards the use of tape-slide learning materials in non-formal education.

It was found that the tryout of the tape-slide programme on 11 to 14 year old girls outside school was effective and that the tape-slide presentation was a viable means of teaching illiterates without assistance of a teacher. It was also found that the teacher-trainees felt that tape-slide materials were useful for making the lesson interesting and more useful in large classes.

Satwant Bhangoo and Amrit Kaur (1995) conducted an "experimental study of the multimedia approach in learning by adult rural women" to assess the effectiveness of multimedia approach.

The findings of the study showed that there were differences in the effectiveness of some of the selected methods and their combinations. The use of the combination of three or two methods have been found to yield higher gain as well as retention of knowledge. The findings of the study also showed that the retention of knowledge increased when the printed material was combined with visual cum oral methods. The most important conclusion that can be drawn from the present study is that multimedia approach is very effective in gaining maximum knowledge.

Shah and Gupta (1986) made a comparative study on "effectiveness of visual aids". A field experiment was undertaken for a comparative study of the effectiveness of these visual aids in imparting non-formal education. Two specific subject areas were chosen for the study. Those were (i) importance of educating girls and women for family, personal development and personal contribution to the family (ii) Importance of supplementary income activities through which women can supplement family's income, benefits women can derive from supplementary income activities. The study armved at certain interesting conclusions.

The major findings were: There was significant difference in the pre-test and post-test scores showing an over all gain in knowledge of educating girls and women, gain in knowledge of supplementary income activities and change in opinion with respect to supplementary income activities in experimental group subjected to flash cards, to puppet and the slides.

Uma Joshi and Anjali Gupta (1993) conducted a study on "effectiveness of video in educating women of low socio economic status". The important findings of the study were:

(i) Video films can be effective in imparting knowledge to the women in non-formal education.

(ii) Video films can be produced on the content relevant to the needs of the various groups of women so that they may be well accepted as one of the effective media for education.

(iii) Since women have shown high interest in income generating activities, such activities can be taken up in various adult education centres run by Home Science Education and Extension Department and other agencies.

(iv) A video film scripted and produced considering all such aspects can ensure its effectiveness.

Critique of the Studies Under this Subhead

When compared with the studies in formal education setting, the studies conducted on multimedia in non formal education setting are not adequate in terms of quantity and variety. A few investigations have been carried out to verify the efficacy of video packages in imparting knowledge to or in creating awareness among rural children or women (Basker, 1990; Bhangoo and Kaur, 1989; Uma Joshi and Anjali Gupta, 1993). Video film ignites high interest in women in income generating activities (Uma Joshi and Anjali Gupta, 1993). Also they make a useful suggestion that such activities can be taken up in various adult education centres run by Home Science Education and Extension Department and other agencies.

Some studies have been conducted on TV programmes pertinent to nonformal education. Whilst some studies attempt to establish the effectiveness of TV programmes on acquisition of knowledge (Cherian, 1986; Kannan, 1976; Kaur and Koshy, 1970;), other studies try to assess the role of TV in creating awareness (Holtzman, 1981; Mody, 1978). TV viewing helped men and women to gain significant amount of knowledge about green vegetables, polio vaccination and leproscopy (Cherian, 1980) but where there is a high rate of illiteracy this development in communication has not brought about significant degree of success (Kannan, 1976). TV viewing added to the retention of knowledge already acquired in non-formal setting (Kaur and Koshy, 1970).

The studies on other visual aids done by Mullick (1981), and Shah and Gupta (1986) also establish the effectiveness of low cost visual aids in non-formal education setting. While the study of Shah and Gupta (1986), verifies the effectiveness of visual aids, the other study (Mullick, 1981) establishes efficacy besides pointing out the attitude of the teachers. It is disheartening to note that adequate studies have not been attempted on affordable technology *i.e.*, print media applicable to rural and non-formal settings.

Studies Conducted on Modular Approach in Formal Education in India

Studies conducted by different researchers on the effectiveness of modular approach in formal education in India are presented under this subheading.

Chelladurai, N. (1994) conducted an experimental study on "impact of modular approach on developing environmental awareness among primary students" with the following objectives:

(1) To identify the competencies to be attained by the students of V Std in environmental science in each area.

(2) To develop self instructional modules to enable students to attain M.L.L. in environmental science.

(3) To find out the effectiveness of modular approach in teaching environmental science at Std V level.

The study arrived at the following conclusions:

(1) There is significant difference between the pre-test and post-test scores of experimental group students.

(2) There is significant difference between the post-test scores of experimental group and control group.

(3) M.L.L. in environmental science could be achieved after modular experimentation to a considerable extent.

Dhamija (1986) made a comparative study of the "effectiveness of three approaches of instructions - conventional, radio vision and modular approach on achievement of students in social studies".

The objectives of the study were:

(i) To compare the achievement of students of class VIII in social studies when taught through three different approaches viz. radio vision, modular and conventional.

(ii) To compare the achievement of students in geography when taught through these three approaches.

(iii) To compare the achievement of students in civics when taught through these three approaches.

(iv) To compare the achievement of students in history when taught through these three approaches.

The study revealed the following:

(i) The students achieved highest knowledge achievement scores in geography when taught through radio vision.

(ii) The achievement of the students was the highest in knowledge achievement scores in civics when taught through the modular approach.

(iii) The students achieved the highest knowledge achievement scores in history when taught through the conventional approach.

(iv) The involvement of students in the classroom was maximum when they were taught through the radio vision approach.

(v) Self-confidence among the students increased most when they were taught through the modular approach.

Gabriel, Pillai and Gnanam (1989) studied the effects of thirteen different kinds of learning strategies in the modular scheduling. They found the modular scheduling to be effective with reference to the high achievers, average achievers and low achievers.

Gabriel and Pillai (1991) in their study 'modularisation - an attempt at collegiate level in India' have established the effectiveness of modules at higher level education.

Hopper (1982) conducted 'an experimental study in the use of modular approach for teaching biology in standard XI'. The main objectives of the study were:

(i) To design and develop instructional modules on selected units in morphology, physiology and ecology for higher secondary classes.

(ii) To find out the relative effectiveness of three modular approaches involving self learning, peer group learning and peer group learning with teacher intervention.

(iii) To compare the cumulative achievements of students through three different sequences of content presentation.

(iv) To find out the effect of different modular courses of study on the academic motivation of students.

(v) To find out the relationship between intelligence and achievement through modular instruction.

The major findings of the study were:

(i) All the three structured modular approaches of teaching were effective in terms of mean gain in cognitive achievement in morphology, physiology and ecology.

(ii) All the three modular approaches were effective for the attainment of mean gain in higher mental abilities with respect to morphology and ecology. But none of them was effective enough as regards physiology.

(iii) The most effective modular course of study with respect to cognitive achievements and retentivity of the content and objectives was that which had the sequence of ecology morphology-physiology.

(iv) Interaction between method and content was significant influencing total achievement.

(v) The modular approach of teaching biology led to a significant increase in the academic motivation of the students.

(vi) There was no relationship between intelligence and mean gain in achievement through modular instruction.

(vii) In total sample, 84 per cent pupils favoured the modular approach involving peer group learning with the teacher available at the time of need.

Jayalakshmi (1985) in her study on "systematising instructional modules in educational psychology at B.Ed. level" and Mukhopadhyay (1981) in his study on 'Micro Teaching versus Modular approach; comparative effectiveness in developing teaching competence" have established the feasibility and effectiveness of modular approach at B.Ed. level.

Mahange, Satoki (1991)—conducted "an investigation of modular instruction in the Tanzanian primary school system."

The purpose of the study was to observe, describe and analyse potential factors that would need to be considered in introducing modular designs for teaming in Tanzanian primary schools.

The findings revealed that although, the modules were effective in teaching geography topics to both rural and urban pupils, the urban pupils benefitted considerably more than those in rural schools. The results also reflected that the pupils who studied the modules under teacher support systems scored higher in the test than those who studied it independently.

Natarajan, N. (1996)—made a study on "effectiveness of modular approach in learning English by the plus two higher secondary students" with the following objectives:

(i) To develop modules for learning English Grammar by the +2 students.

(ii) To find out the achievement of Hr. Sec. students in learning English grammar while taught through modular approach.

(iii) To find out the achievement of the boys and girls taught through modular approach.

The major findings of the study are given below:

(i) Modular approach significantly improved the achievement of students after modular treatment.

(ii) Sex has not influenced the performance of the boys and girls taught through modular approach.

(iii) The boys and girls taught through modular approach showed better performance than the boys and girls taught through traditional lecture method.

Reddy and Ramar (1994) studied the "effectiveness of multimedia based modules in teaching social science to low achievers". The study concluded that the multimedia based modules enabled the experimental group low achievers to show a significantly higher performance in the post-test. While the rate of progress shown by the control group was 14.9 per cent, the rate of progress shown by the experimental group low achievers was 70.3 per cent. Though there existed a gulf of difference between the experimental group and the normal group in the pre-test, the gap was narrowed down to a very great extent by the experimental group low achievers in the post-test. It signifies that the multimedia based modular approach could enable the experimental group low achievers to cope with normal students to a considerable extent.

Reddy and Ramar (1995) assessed the "effectiveness of multimedia based modular approach in teaching of maths to low achievers". After analysis, the study arrived at the following conclusions.

(i) Though the control group and experimental group lowachievers were alike in the pre-test, the experimental group low achievers could surge far ahead of control group low achievers in the post-test.

(ii) While the control group low achievers could not narrow down the gap that existed between them and the normal group students, the experimental group low achievers could narrow down the gap to a considerable extent due to multimedia modular treatment. This substantiates the advantage of multimedia based modular approach over traditional lecture method.

(iii) In terms of progress and rate of progress, it is the experimental group low achievers who excelled the other two groups. It testifies to the effectiveness of multimedia based modules in teaching maths to low achievers.

Reddy and Ramar (1995) undertook an experimental study to measure the "effectiveness of multimedia based modular approach in teaching science to low achievers". The detailed analysis of the study gave the following conclusions.

(i) The low achievers found the multimedia based modules very effective in learning science. The modules very much catered to individual differences.

(ii) It enabled the experimental group low achievers to evince a performance par excellence in the post-test. Their post-test performance was far ahead of control group low achievers.

(iii) The experimental group low achievers showed a better rate of progress than the control group low achievers and the normal group students. This fact vouches for the effectiveness of multimedia based modules.

(iv) The control group low achievers could not diminish the gulf of difference that existed between them and the normal group students. But, the experimental group low achievers could not only narrow down the gap that existed between them and the normal group students, but also they could reach the pre-test mean score of the normal group students. This exalts the advantage of multimedia based modular approach over the traditional lecture method.

Sahajahan (1980) conducted "an experimental study on teaching science in Standard VI and VII through modules". The objectives of the investigation were:

(i) To design and develop modules for teaching science in standards VI and VII.

(ii) To study the effectiveness of the modules as an instructional method with respect to the conventional method.

(iii) To study the relationship between the students' achievement through modules and the attitude of the students towards the module as well as academic motivation of the students.

(iv) To compare the achievements through modules of high achievers and low achievers, boys and girls, high academic motivation and low academic motivation and the like.

The major findings of the investigation were:

(i) The modular way of learning was more effective than the conventional method in the case of some modules while in the case of other modules it was found as effective as the conventional method.

(ii) An overwhelming majority of the students possessed a favourable attitude towards modular instruction and their attitude was stable throughout the period of experimentation.

(iii) The teachers' reactions to modular approach to instruction were favourable.

(iv) The achievement of the students through instructional modules seemed to have a low positive correlation with their attitude towards modular way of learning.

(v) While learning through modules, no significant difference was found between the achievements of extremely high and extremely low achievers and between girls and boys.

(vi) The attitudes of students towards instructional modules, academic motivation of students and their reading comprehension were not related to one another.

Thalaimalai, R. (1996) studied the "effectiveness of multimedia based modular approach in teaching botany at higher secondary level". The study concluded that this multimedia based modular approach was more effective than traditional lecture method in teaching botany to plus one students. This multimedia modular treatment was more effective to below average students, moderately effective to average students and not so significantly effective to above average students as it was to the students of the other two groups. The study also pointed out that concrete presentation of subject content, direct experience and learner's involvement could be ensured in this approach.

Critique of the Studies Under this Subhead

Though adequate researches have not been carried out in this area, there are some studies which differ from one another in purpose and range. Studies conducted on effectiveness of modular instruction at primary level establish that this approach has a positive impact on achievement of students (Chelladurai, 1994; Mahange and Satoki, 1991) and it is more effective to urban children than rural children (Mahange and Satoki, 1991). Reddy and Ramar (1994, 1995a, 1995b, 1996, 1997) and Sahajahan (1980) have verified the efficacy of modules in teaching science, maths and social science at higher elementary level. Modular instruction has had significant effect on achievement of students in Botany and English at higher secondary level. (Hopper, 1982; Natarajan, 1996; Thalaimalai, 1996). Efficacy of modular instruction at college level has been established and it is found to be effective in reaching out to all the students (Gabriel, Pillai and Gnanam, 1989; Gabriel and Pillai, 1991; Jayalakshmi, 1985; Mukhopadhyay, 1991).

There is a striking agreement among studies in establishing that modular instruction is very effective in reaching out to all the students. Also, it enables low achievers or below average students to cope with average and above average students to a considerable extent (Gabriel, Pillai and Gnanam, 1989; Reddy and Ramar, 1994, 1995a 1995b, 1996, 1997; Sahajahan, 1980; Thalaimalai, 1996). This approach is very effective in motivating and in developing self confidence in the students and the reaction of the teacher and the attitude of the students are found to be favourable (Dhamija, 1986; Hopper, 1982; Sahajahan, 1980). Some critical questions such as how to give the students the entire book in modular form, how to meet out the cost and how to budget time are not clearly clarified though a feeble attempt has been made by Reddy and Ramar (1994, 1995a, 1995b) who state that the modular version of the textbook can be given to students in the form of a handbook like Teachers Handbook'.

Adequate studies are yet to be attempted to establish the efficacy of modular instruction in teaching various subjects at school level and also at higher level.

Studies Conducted on Modular Approach in Non- formal Education in India

Quite a few studies have been conducted to assess the effectiveness of modular approach in non-formal education in India. Such studies are summed up under this sub-head.

Chopra (1988) made an experimental study on "developing learning packages and testing their effectiveness on illiterate adults". In the study he concluded that learning material in the form of modules was helpful to the adult learners in attaining literacy, numeracy and social skills. He also found that the male and female adults might have achievement differently in spite of the same modules.

Kundu (1985) in his study on "adult education numeracy modules" have brought to light the effectiveness of modules and he has highlighted the effectiveness of modules in learning numbers.

Rita Chopra (1992) conducted a study on "effect of teaching modules on achievement scores of male and female adults". The main objectives of the study were:

(i) To develop modules for adult learners.

(ii) To test the effectiveness of the developed modules.

(iii) To find out the quantitative and qualitative effectiveness of the modules.

The results of her study show that the adult learners had attained literacy, numeracy and social awareness after their exposure to modules. However, the female and male adults showed variation on different aspects of the module. This has an implication for the adult education functionaries to develop and use modules for adult teaching. The researchers need to test the effectiveness of the module on different samples.

Critique of the Studies Under this Subhead

Only a few studies have been conducted in non-formal education setting in India. Also, these studies have been carried out with reference to adult learners (Chopra, 1988; Kundu, 1985; Rita Chopra, 1992). These studies verify the effectiveness of modules in teaching adult learners. Learning modules are very helpful to the adult learners in attaining literacy, numeracy and social skills (Chopra, 1988; Kundu, 1985; Rita Chopra, 1992). There is difference between male and female in their achievement after their exposure to modular instruction. (Chopra, 1988; Rita Chopra, 1992). Modules are specifically very effective in learning numbers (Kundu 1985).

Though Chopra (1983) and Rita Chopra (1992) have established the effectiveness of modular instruction in learning/ attaining literacy, numeracy and social skills, they have not made any attempt to study the relative efficacy of modular instruction with special reference to attainment of each skill. Also, there are various categories in non-formal education. But the aforesaid studies have been carried out in the area of adult education. This area also needs further probe at micro level while the other areas warrant the immediate attention of researchers and educators so that this modular strategy which has been found to be very effective in reaching out to all the students, can be made available to the students in those areas. There is a greater need to apply this modular instruction to the young learners in non-formal sector and its effectiveness should be assessed.

Studies Conducted on Low Achievers and Slow Learners in India

Some studies on low achievers and a very few studies on slow learners have been done in India. Studies related to low achievers and slow learners are presented under this sub-head.

Deka (1985) conducted "a causal comparative study of high and low achievers' to find out the causative factors behind the academic success or failure of the students by mainly comparing the characteristics of the high and low achievers.

The major findings were:

(i) Low achievers always performed poorly in their school examinations and had greater incidence of school failures. Low proficiency in certain basic subjects such as vocabulary, spelling, arithmetic and general knowledge was significantly and positively related to school failure.

(ii) School failure was significantly and positively related to general mental ability. Intelligence of high and low achievers, was not affected by residence and sex. Low scholastic achievement was significantly and positively associated with inferior leadership quality and less adventurousness.

(iii) School success and failure were significantly and positively related to family income, involvement in domestic activities and home study, while they were unrelated to parental education and occupation.

(iv) School failure was positively associated with school attendance, preparation of school work, understanding of lesson, preparation for examinations, favourable attitude of teachers and early school leaving.

(v) School failure gave rise to unfavourable attitude towards teacher and two major subjects of study—English and mathematics.

Girija Devi Thampuratty (1994) explored the socio-economic status of creative high achievers and creative low achievers in mathematics with the following objective:

To explore whether the socio-economic status variables namely parental income, parental occupation and level of parental education were related to achievement in mathematics of pupils high in creativity. The revealings of the study were:

(i) Students of parents having high income, of high profession and having high education are more creative and achieve higher than students of parents having low income, of low profession and low education.

(ii) The mean scores of parental income, parental occupation and parental education of creative high achievers are significantly higher than those of the creative low achievers.

Janakkumar (1996) conducted a study on the "effectiveness of remedial packages for learning the active skills in English by the low achievers at secondary level". The study aimed at measuring the effectiveness of the remedial packages in enabling the low achievers to cope with the normal students in learning active skills in English. The results of the study proved the remedial package treatment in teaching English to be more effective than the traditional lecture method to the low achievers in class IX.

Khan, S. A. (1983) conducted a study of the personality characteristics of educationally backward pupils of Hr. Sec. Schools of Lucknow District with the following objectives:

(i) To discover the significant variables of personality responsible for low achievement, and

(ii) To find out the relationship between these variables. The study arrived at the following conclusions:

 (i) Educationally backward pupils were more reserved, detached and aloof, less intelligent, more emotionally unstable, more excitable and impatient, timid and threat-sensitive, tender minded and sensitive, more internally reflective, more insecure, worrying and guilt-prone, socially group dependent, uncontrolled and careless of social rules, over-wrought and frustrated.

 (ii) On second order factors the educationally backward pupils were more introverts, tender minded and subdued and had more anxiety and poor adjustment.

 (iii) It was also found that the hampering effects of aloofness, emotional instability, excitability, aggression, dominance, guilt proneness, feeling of insecurity, tension and frustration etc., were more prevalent at the adolescent stage (13 to 16 years) than at the preadolescent stage (10 to 12 years.)

Koul (1978) conducted a study on 'personality needs of high and low achievers in mathematics'. The major findings of the study were:

(i) The high achievers in mathematics differed significantly from low achievers on eighth of Murrays needs.

(ii) Several scales of EPPS discriminated between the high and low achievers in mathematics and could be used as possible non-academic predictors of achievement in mathematics.

Kumaraiah (1976) undertook an investigation into the "intellectual, personal and social factors related to high and low achievement of various stages in medical education". The objective of the investigation was to study the said factors in relation to high and low achievement at pre-professional, pre-clinical and para-clinical stages in undergraduate medical education.

The following were the findings of the study:

(i) Out of the fifty one factors (intellectual and non-intellectual) studied, thirty eight factors, thirty six being non-intellectual, significantly differentiated the high and the low achievers at some stages.

(ii) Four factors, namely, intelligence, health adjustment, emotional adjustment and overall general adjustment consistently differentiated the high and low achievers at all stages in undergraduate medical education.

Mishra (1978) conducted 'a comparative study of high and low achievers in science, commerce and arts on creativity, intelligence and anxiety'. The findings of the study were:

(i) The high achievers in arts were higher on the level of creativity than the low achievers in arts.

(ii) The high achievers in commerce were higher as regards the level of creativity than the low achievers in that stream.

(iii) The high achievers in science were higher on the level of creativity than their low achieving counterparts.

Similarly the higher achievers in arts, commerce and science groups were higher in their level of intelligence than their low achieving counterparts. The science students were more creative, intelligent and low in general anxiety than their counterparts in other streams. The arts students were low in creativity and intelligence but high in general anxiety. The science students exhibited more creative talent and low general quality.

B. Prasanna, K.C.B., (1984) made a study of certain mental health variables associated with high and low achieving adolescents.

The findings of the study indicated the need:

(i) to avoid threats which cause disequilibrium in children.

(ii) to provide for guidance oriented teaching

(iii) to organise extension lectures for parents & community leaders.

(iv) to form parent teacher associations and

(v) to encourage pupils to participate in extra curricular activities and institutional guidance.

Pushpita John (1977) studied "some socio-personal attitudes related to high and low academic performance of secondary school leavers" with the objective to identify certain attitudinal variables that would discriminate between high and low achievers in secondary schools.

The major findings were:

(i) The attitudinal variables which seemed to have the highest potency in discriminating high and low achievers were self-effort vs. fatalism, other acceptance, independence vs. conformity, future, present and past.

(ii) The attitudes, which seemed to have least effectiveness, were risk taking, authority and radicalism.

(iii) All the variables were found to be useful in discriminating between at least one or the other of the subgroups of extreme achievers compared.

"A comparative study of a few differential personality correlates of low and high achievers" was made by Raj (1974).

The following were the conclusions of the study:

(i) Anxiety as a personality trait had a changing role in scholastic achievement.

(ii) Low level of anxiety helped in achieving high, whereas very high level of anxiety was detrimental to achievement.

(iii) Level of aspiration was not a significant correlative of achievement

(iv) Low goal setting was in no way a desirable characteristic for better achievement

Reddy and Ramar (1995) undertook a study to assess the 'effectiveness of computer assisted instruction in teaching science to slow learners'. After the experiment, the slow learners in the experimental group evinced better mean gain than the control group slow learners. Also, they could narrow down the gap between them and the normal group students. The narrowed down gap between both the groups may be ascribed to the effectiveness of CAI. But the authors are silent over the feasibility of CAI in Indian school setting where most of the schools do not have even a single computer.

Reddy and Ramar (1996a) conducted an experimental study on 'relative effectiveness of video instruction in teaching science and social science to slow learners'. The study established the effectiveness of video instruction in teaching science and social science to slow learners. There was better rate of progress in social science than in science. This strategy enabled the experimental group slow learners to cope with normal students to a considerable extent

Reddy and Ramar (1996b) assessed impact of modular approach on achievement of slow learners in Social Science. The study concluded that modular approach was very effective in reaching out to all the students. This strategy also enabled the slow learners to cope with normal students to a considerable extent. Since it happens to be an affordable technology for all, more researches of this kind need to be undertaken with a view to design our instructional programme so as to reach out to all the students.

Reddy and Ramar (1996) have described certain procedures to identify slow learners which have been successfully used in Indian school setting. They recommend identification of slow learners on the basis of a three phase process which is more feasible and more reliable. This process incorporates both informal measures like observation, educational assessment etc. and formal assessment measures like standardised tests. These two assessment measures complement each other. Also, they point out that Sandra's checklist can be used to counter check the initially identified slow learners.

Reddy and Ramar (1997a) assessed 'effectiveness of multimedia based modular approach in teaching English to slow learners'. The study found this strategy to be effective in teaching English to the slow learners. This approach had a positive impact on the retention of slow learners. They also suggested how this strategy could be used to boost up the achievement of slow learners so as to diminish wastage and stagnation in our schools. Further, they have described how this approach can be used so as to reach out to all the students.

Reddy and Ramar (1997b) undertook an experimental study to verify the effectiveness of multimedia instructional strategy in teaching science to slow learners.

The obtained results showed that the multimedia instructional strategy was more effective than the traditional lecture method in teaching science and it enabled the slow learners to cope with normal students to a considerable extent The study also furnishes a wide ranging list of further researches to be undertaken with special reference to slow learners.

The study also points out the applicability and feasibility of multimedia instructional strategy in Indian school setting.

Reddy, Ramar and Kusuma (1997) have dealt with the learning problems of slow learning children and they expound how to teach language and mathematics to slow learners. Also, they have furnished a variety of educational programmes for slow learners. Further, they provide means and methods to develop social competence in slow learners. Their work encompasses the problems of slow learners from primary level to adulthood and provides appropriate intervention strategies to circumvent specific deficiency. These authors seem to have set out to give the intellectual grounding and practical strategies to the present and tomorrow's teachers to make them become more effective instructors of slow learners.

Saun (1980) made a study on 'pattern of disclosure and adjustment among high and low achievers'.

The important findings were:

(i) Self disclosure pattern of the high and low adjusted male adolescents was significantly different in three areas namely, money, study and interest.

(ii) High and low achieving adolescents showed different adjustment pattern in home, social and emotional areas.

(iii) The female high and low achievers were more or less equally communicative except in the areas of study.

Singh (1983) made a 'comparative study of high and low academic achievers in self-concept formation'.

The findings of the study were:

(i) A positively significant relationship was found between self concept and academic achievement of arts, science and commerce students.

(ii) The relationship between academic achievement and self concept of art students was significantly higher than that of science and commerce and total students.

(iii) There was a significant difference in the self concept of high and low academic achievers in favour of high achievers.

(iv) No significant difference was found in the self concept of urban male and female high achievers.

(v) Urban girls belonging to low academic achievement were found to have better self concept than their male counterparts.

(vi) Self concept and academic achievement were significantly better in the case of female than of male students.

(vii) Urban students had better academic achievement than rural students, whereas, they were at par in self respect.

Singh (1986) made 'a study of some possible contributing factors to high and low achievement in mathematics of the high school students of Orissa'. The main findings were:

(i) Achievement in mathematics was positively and significantly related to intelligence, SES and study attitudes.

(ii) Intelligence, study attitude and SES contributed in this order of importance to discrimination between the high and low achieving groups.

Singh (1984) conducted a survey of the study habits of high, middle, and low achieving adolescents in relation to their sex, intelligence and socio-economic status. The main findings of the study were:

(i) Adolescent boys had significantly better study habits than adolescent girls.

(ii) Study habits were significantly related to academic achievement. High achieving adolescents had significantly better study habits than middle achievers who, in turn, had significantly better study habits than low achievers.

(iii) Study habits of adolescent boys and girls differed significantly at different levels of intelligence, *i.e.*, high, middle and low.

(iv) Study habits of adolescent boys and girls differed significantly at different levels of socio economic status, *i.e.*, high, middle and low.

(v) Intelligence and socio economic status did not interact significantly in relation to the study habits of either adolescent boys or girls.

(vi) The triple interaction among academic achievement, intelligence and socio economic status was not significant in relation to the study of either adolescent boys or girls.

A. Singh, K.K. (1995) studied some personality factors of high and low intelligent boys and girls of Bhagalpur. The study concluded that high intelligent males were scholastic, emotionally mature, conscientious, venturesome and controlled. High intelligent girls were scholastic, controlled and shrewd. Low intelligent boys were outgoing, emotionally immature, assertive, happy go lucky and imaginative. Low intelligent girls were outgoing, less scholastic and apprehensive.

Somasundaram (1980) conducted 'a comparative study of certain personality variables related to over-normal and under achievement in secondary school mathematics'. The study shows that the variables of social standards, introversion, family relations, test anxiety and community relations discriminated between under achievers and non under achievers.

Sontakey, (1986) conducted 'a comparative study of personality factors and achievement motivation of high and low achievers in natural and biological sciences'. The major findings of the study were:

(i) High achievers were more intelligent, less excitable tough minded, self reliant and realistic than the low achievers as groups in biological sciences.

(ii) High achievers were more intelligent, less excitable than the low achievers.

(iii) The achievement motivation as measured by G. Rao's achievement motivation test was a poor predictor of achievement in biological and natural sciences.

(iv) The socio economic status and sex of high and low achievers did not interact with each other to bring about differences in achievement motivation of the subject.

(v) The socio economic status and high achievement motivation had positive association with achievement in both biological and natural sciences.

(vi) Personality factors were consistently associated with achievement in natural as well as biological sciences.

(vii) Education of mothers was found particularly operative in bringing about high achievement.

Soundararaja Rao and Rajaguru (1995) studied "effectiveness of video assisted instruction on the achievement of slow learners". The major objectives of the study are:

(i) To investigate the effectiveness of video assisted instructions on the achievement of slow learners in learning science concepts.

(ii) To make a comparative study of the achievement of slow learners in terms of the following variables: sex difference, socio-economical difference, management of school, parents' educational status and family size of slow learners.

(iii) To study the relationship between achievement of slow learners and their intellectual capacity.

After analysis, the study gave the following conclusions:

(i) The slow learners of control and experimental groups were alike in immediate retention. But female slow learners of video assisted instruction group performed better in immediate retention than conventional learning group.

(ii) Irrespective of the type of schools managed by different bodies, the slow learners of those groups were alike in immediate retention.

(iii) The socio-economic status had impact on immediate retention of slow learners in learning science concepts through video assisted instruction.

(iv) The video assisted instruction facilitated male and female slow learners to have better retention even after the lapse of one month period.

(v) The socio-economic status had impact on retention test with regard to experimental group slow learners. On the other hand, the remaining factors like parent's educational status and family size have least impact on retention test.

(vi) The male and female slow learners in control and experimental groups were alike in intelligence test.

(vii) The slow learners of Government schools and private schools were alike in intelligence test.

(viii) The socio-economic status and parent's educational status had least impact on intelligence of control and experimental group slow learners.

(ix) The intellectual ability of slow learners was positively correlated with post-test and retention test. The correlation between post-test and retention test was also positive.

Subramanyam and Ramadevi (1991) explored "some differential characteristics of high and low achievers in secondary schools". The objective of the study was to examine the differences between high and low achievers with regard to their (i) intelligence (ii) creative talent (iii) reading ability and achievement motivation.

The following were the conclusions:

(i) The high achievers possess higher level of mental ability and low achievers possess low intelligence. The scholastic attainment and intelligence were closely related to each other.

(ii) The high achievers exhibit a higher level of creative talent whereas the low achievers do not.

(iii) The high achievers possess better reading skills compared to low achievers.

(iv) The high achievers are highly motivated towards achievement. The low achievers were not so motivated towards achievement.

Sumangala (1995) investigated. "some psychological variables discriminating between high and low achievers in mathematics". The objective of this study was to see whether some psychological variables like mathematics aptitude (and its components), attitude towards maths and self concept in mathematics could discriminate significantly between high and low achievers in mathematics and if so, to find the extent of relation of these variables with achievement in mathematics.

The main findings were:

(i) High achievers and low achievers were significantly different with regard to each of the independent variables.

(ii) The mathematics aptitude of high achievers is favourable when compared to that of the low achievers and the self-concept in mathematics of high achievers is 'higher' when compared to that of the low achievers in mathematics.

(iii) Achievement in mathematics is related not only to cognitive variables like intelligence, aptitude etc., but also to the effective variables like attitude towards mathematics and self-concept in mathematics.

Critique of the Studies Under this Sub-head

Most of the studies on low achievement are survey studies. These studies can be categorised into two broad types as studies related to the personality factors of high and low achievers and studies related to factors contributing to high and low achievement. Some survey studies indicate that educationally backward pupils were more reserved, less intelligent, more emotionally unstable, more excitable and impatient, more internally reflective and less motivated (Khan, 1983; Singh, 1995; Sontakey, 1986; Subramaniam and Ramadevi, 1991). The comparative studies made on high and low achievers are mostly in agreement with one another. The studies show social standards, introversion, family relations, test anxiety, community relations, creativity, intelligence, self-concept discriminated between high and low achievers (Mishra, 1978; Somasundaram, 1980; Subramaniam and Ramadevi, 1991; Sumangala, 1995). The second category studies indicate that intellectual, personal, social factors, study attitude, interest and involvement were some causative factors for high and low achievement (Deka, 1985; Saun, 1980; Singh, 1986; Singh, 1995;). Only a few experimental studies have been carried out to assess the efficacy of certain instructional strategies with special reference to low achievers (Janakkumar, 1996; Ramar, 1994).

As for studies on slow learners, there is no other book exclusively on slow learners except the one by Reddy, Ramar/ and Kusuma (1997). Most of the studies done so far attempt to assess the efficacy of one instructional strategy or the other with special reference to slow learners (Reddy and Ramar, 1995; 1996a; 1996b, 1997a; 1997b;). Attempt has been made to assess the relative effectiveness of a particular strategy *i.e.*, video instruction with special reference to more than one subject (Reddy and Ramar, 1996a) It has been established that video instruction is very effective in ensuring immediate retention (Reddy and Ramar, 1997a; Soundararaja Rao and Rajaguru, 1995). Survey studies are warranted to identify the personality characteristics of slow learners and other variables causing slow learning.

STUDIES DONE ABROAD

Studies related to the problems under investigation conducted in foreign countries are presented as under.

Studies Conducted Abroad on Multimedia in Education

Quite a number of studies have been conducted on multimedia in foreign countries. Some of the related studies are summed up under this sub-head.

Adebola Dekoya, Jones A. Akangbe (1992) conducted a study on "use of instructional methods and media technology in training of extension managers and supervisors in Nigeria. The main objectives of the study were:

(i) To determine the frequency of use, obstacle to use and felt training need in the use of instructional media resources and technology.

(ii) To compare the perceptions of two respondent groups of management trainers concerning the three areas of investigation.

The important findings of the study were:

(i) The two respondent groups tended to be mutually agreed on six of the ten obstacles to the use of instructional media and technology for the training of extension managers and supervisors at the Agricultural and Rural Management Training Institute. The respondent groups considered not only those obstacles that are present within the system or organisation but also those that the training institute has no control over.

(ii) The two respondent groups only differed in one area of training need. The respondent group of faculty members with five or more years of experience in the use of audio-visual equipment differed significantly from the group with lesser years in their perception of the training need in the use of video tape recorder/player for conducting course and programmes.

(iii) Incidentally, microcomputer is ranked first, among the audio-visual equipment, and the respondents sought highest training in their use.

(iv) The two respondent groups consider added training in the use of microcomputer as useful for improving their efficiency on the job or in the way they conduct training programmes and sessions.

Altbach (1982) surveyed higher education in the 3rd world. He came out with valuable findings of the global pattern of knowledge dissemination and how it affects the 3rd world. He noted that the 3rd world Countries had shortage of books, journals, films, travels for students. There were also the problems of writing text books, trained teachers and other teaching materials.

Baggalcy and Duck (1974) conducted six experiments, in each of which the effects of a particular television production technique were examined. Their studies indicated that a number of basic production procedures influence the psychological impact of ETV material powerfully and quite unwittingly. Their studies offered specific guidelines for more deliberate control by television producers in future.

The specific results of their six experiments are as follows:

(i) The edited insertion of varying audience reaction shots significantly affected the performer's perceived popularity and interest value, expertise and intelligibility.

(ii) The electronic insertion of a picture background significantly increased the performer's perceived credibility—more honest profound, reliable and fair.

(iii) The re-recording and edited insertion of the interviewer's role in a discussion significantly increased his perceived sincerity, tension and intelligibility.

(iv) The re-recording and edited insertion of the interviewer's role in a discussion favourably increased the impact of the interview also.

(v) When a performer was framed, so that his notes were visible, he was related less fair and more confusing than when the notes were not visible.

The results suggested that the major emphasis of previous media research on factors of programme content (*i.e.*, subject matter) had been misguided, since the audience's interpretation of content may itself be affected by the presentation strategies mediating it.

Benaloh, Lauril Anne Blake (1994) conducted a study entitled "teachers, students and instructional software: What works, well when and why". This research was an exploratory study based on teacher and student evaluations of different teaching styles while using instructional software. Three teaching styles (monitoring, co-ordinating and mediating) were used with each of three software packages in three grade 5 classes. The classroom teachers and 18 students, selected to represent different preferred learning styles were interviewed as to what they felt were the advantages and disadvantages of each style/software dyad.

Contrary to expectations, the effectiveness of the three styles did not seem to depend on the primary instructional style of the teacher or on the preferred learning styles of the students. Rather, these results suggested that, for optimal effectiveness, all three styles should be used with every instructional software programme. The mediating style provides a demonstration of software, allows the teacher to highlight the important concepts, and shows the students what achievement is possible. Co-ordinated activities provide additional time and contexts for students to learn the concepts. The monitoring style shows students to work with the concepts at their own pace. Demonstrating these styles to teachers in their classes seemed very useful for encouraging them to use the styles themselves.

Borras Isabel (1993) conducted a study to assess "effects of subtitled video during transactional task practice on oral communicative performance of fifth semester college students of French learning with multi-media course ware". The purpose of this study was to investigate the effectiveness of subtitled video during transactional task practice on oral communicative performance of fifth semester college students of French learning with multimedia course ware. The major findings are:

(i) Subjects in the subtitles treatment scored significantly higher on the oral performance measure and had significantly better attitudes than the subjects in the no sub-titles treatments.

(ii) The effects of task level and the interaction of these variables with subtitling were significant.

Butts and Prikets (1969) compared the effectiveness of tape slides material in audio-tutorial laboratories and conventional teaching as done in traditional laboratories based on students achievement in accounting principles. The tape slide material group (experimental group) received traditional instruction and audio-tutorial laboratory materials consisting of tape slide materials and assignment exercise. The control group received traditional instruction as given in the laboratories without the use of tape slide materials. The experimental group achieved better than the control group in accounting achievement test.

Chotam *et al.*, (1986) studied "educational television and the curriculum for children upto the age of seven years".

The studies in England and Wales showed that educational television was used by 259 teachers of children upto the age of seven years. It indicated that only a few teachers were using the medium effectively for class viewing and mass viewing of programmes.

Dobbins, E. Renee, (1994) undertook a study to measure the effectiveness of "math computer assisted instruction with remedial students and students with mild learning/behaviour disabilities". The purpose of the study was to compare the performance of third and fourth grade students with mild learning/behaviour disabilities and selected third and fourth grade students without mild learning/behaviour disabilities when using the computerized programme, "math concepts and skills" as measured by the in-line analysis provided by the programme. The major findings of .the study were:

(i) There was a statistically significant difference between the gain scores of students with mild learning/behaviour disabilities and students in the chapter I programme when repeated measurement of gain scores were analysed over the three month period.

(ii) There was a statistically significant difference within tho group of students in the chapter I programme when repeated measurement of gain scores were analysed over the three month period.

(iii) There was no statistically significant interaction between the two groups of students and time when repeated measurement of gain scores were analysed over the three month period.

Elmore, Patricia Venshew (1992) made "an analysis of fifty one computer modules designed to enhance the knowledge, skills, and attitudes needed by teacher education students". This study analyses and reports the findings of students' reactions to a set of 51 computer modules called Performance

Element Modules (PEMs). These modules focussed on selected knowledge, skills and attitudes needed by teacher education students. The main objective was to assess whether students will accept the 51 computer-assisted modules as viable instructional tools.

The major findings revealed a mean scores of 7.73 for "user friendliness" of the computer. For involvement and interaction of the computer programme (modules), a mean score of 7.3 was reported. Did the modules help students correct a lack of information or improve a skill? A mean of 7.12 was reported which was interpreted as an indication that the modules were viable instructional aids.

Fluitman (1990) conducted a study on "training for work in the informal sector: an agenda item for the 1990's". He concluded that the difference in perception after training need in the use of video-tape recorder/player for conducting courses and programmes may be adduced to their individual orientation to the use of audio-visual equipment. Thus, he emphasised the need and effectiveness of multimedia technology in imparting training to the supervisors.

Foxall and Tom (1972) undertook a study on "closed circuit television in training for teaching in Further Educational Institution" at the University College in Cardiff. Their findings are as follows:

(i) Students and tutors were very impressed by the possibilities of the use of closed-circuit television in training, even when they suggested modifications.

(ii) The students saw their main problem as being nervousness because of cameras, lights equipment generally. But, nervousness tended to disappear as the recordings progressed.

(iii) The most valuable single aspect of the exercise was the confidence and insight which students gained from actually seeing them. It was mainly for this reason that students and tutors alike were anxious to use much more recording in future.

Himmelwelt et.al., (1958) in the U.K. conducted a study on 4,500 children of two age groups, 10 to 11 and 13 to 14, in four cities. They took a group of viewers with television sets and another group of non-viewers matched in sex, age, intelligence and social class.

The study revealed that the influence of television on children's leisure, interest, knowledge, outlook and values was much less colourful than it was expected.

Lee (1970) has made a reference to the experiment in the United States in 1970 that was designed to develop a television programme to create interest in pre-school children.

The study showed that the children could remember the names of every toy or soap advertised. The team responsible for preparing the pre-school television programme, studied carefully the methods used by the commercial advertising agencies and developed a new programme entitled "see some street" which adopted the repetitive visual and fast paced commercial techniques to teach letters and numbers to the pre-school children. The programmes were designed to improve reasoning language and numerical skills of the pre-school children living in the improvised areas.

Leitner, Rona Karan (1992) in the study "comparing the effects on reading comprehension of educational video, direct experience, and print" investigated if the effects of educational video approximated the effects of direct experience on reading comprehension for high and low ability readers.

The significant findings were that the educational video was more effective than a traditional lesson for all ability levels, the video lesson generated a larger effect size than the hands-on lesson for low ability readers and there was no difference in the effect between the video lesson for low ability readers and the traditional lesson for high ability readers. Overall the study offered some support for the use of educational video as a pre reading activity to provide prior knowledge and thereby increase reading comprehension, particularly for low ability readers. It also demonstrated that the educational video may be used as a vicarious substitute for direct hands-on experience.

Luisa Livia (1991) undertook "a study of the effects of technology training on teacher productivity and empowerment". The findings depict numerous significant changes in the participants' concerns, usage, comfort, empowerment, productivity and efficiency. Each variable demonstrated a positive effect on teachers' overall feelings of increased productivity. The training generated confidence, creativity, pride and a renewed professionalism in their abilities to produce efficient, accurate, attractive, and effective instructional materials.

Naggy, Linda Farinclli (1992) made "a study of the introduction of interactive video into the secondary science curriculum: A case study using an instruction design model". The purpose of this study was to investigate and document a project designed to introduce interactive video technology into the secondary science curriculum at North Alleghency School District.

The results of the study imply that, because of the complexity of this innovation, teachers in a typical school setting may not have the amount of time or expertise required for development of interactive video materials. Although teachers are anxious to use this technology when they are made aware of its potential, districts may have to look to outside sources for development of appropriate materials if interactive video is to enjoy widespread use in educational settings.

Nishino, Alan Koki (1994) undertook "an exploratory investigation to determine the effects of a multimedia computer-based science learning environment and gender differences, on achievement and attitudes and interests of students in an eighth-grade science classroom". This study employed an exploratory investigative approach which utilized a quantitative two-by-two experimental factorial design. An analysis of co-variance was utilised to adjust for any initial differences. The purpose of the study was to determine the relationship of a multimedia computer based science learning environment and gender differences on achievement and attitudes and interests of students in an eighth grade science classroom. The control group received instruction based upon traditional science teaching methodologies while the experimental group received instruction using a multimedia computer based science learning environment. The following relationships were found.

(i) students in the experimental classroom had a significantly higher post-test mean score in 'self concept' than the students in the traditional science classroom.

(ii) Female students in the experimental classroom had a significantly higher post-test mean score on "self perception as a student" than both the males and females of the traditional science classroom and the males of the experimental classroom.

(iii) Students in the experimental classroom had a significantly higher post-test mean score on the Hueneme Computerised Instruction Test on science than the students in the traditional classroom.

Onah (1970) conducted a comparative study in which 106 students learnt the principles of accounting. The students were randomly assigned to two groups; experimental and control. The experimental group received individual instruction in currels, in audio-visual tutorial laboratory using tape and slides. Additional assistance was available from a tutor at students' convenience. The control group was taught by the conventional method. The establishment of Educational Technology Centres in a number of African countries has taken place recently. Countries such as Ethiopia and Nigeria organise educational broadcasting and television programmes.

Postlethwat, Novak and Murray (1964) report learning efficiency from the use of multimedia teaching strategies. They investigated the possibilities of helping students of meagre background to pursue the study of Botany and at the same time to keep up with their peers. This was arranged originally by making available supplementary tape lectures. The obvious advantage was that it allowed slower students to listen repeatedly to tapes for the purpose of learning, clarifying, or reviewing materials. This procedure led gradually to the development of self tutorial learning experiences which included 8 m.m. film loops and laboratory demonstrations which permitted the individual to make detailed and expected observations. Significant gains in the acquisition of information and desired behavioural changes were reported.

Regser, Gail Renee (1991) conducted a study on "effects of computer education on students achievement, attitude and self-esteem". This study was designed to:

(a) examine the effects of computer education on students' achievement, attitude and self-esteem and

(b) investigate the relationship between success with computer instruction and personality characteristics, IQ, age and attitude towards school.

The major findings of the study are:

(i) There were interesting student gains in effective areas such as attitude and self esteem. Students receiving computer instruction agreed more strongly with positive attitude statements.

(ii) There were no sex related differences in achievement, attitude and personality characteristics.

Robert, Michael, R. (1994) made a "comparison in the effectiveness of the delivery of an Interactive Computer-Assisted Instruction module to a traditional lecture/lab delivered module".

This study examined the use of a computer based multi-media interactive learning system to determine if the learning of a conceptual predictive technological concept was more effective with Interactive Computer Assisted Instruction (ICAI) or with Traditional Instruction (TI). The main finding was: That learners in the experimental group (ICAI) that scored 3 or 37.3 per cent (19/51) on the pre-test had a significantly higher adjusted mean post-test score than learners in the control group.

Schmidt, Susan Carol (1991) made a study on "technology for the 21st century: The effects of an Integrated distributive computer net work system on student achievement". The effects of an integrated distributive computer network system with Wasatch ILS courseware on reading, math and language achievement of sixth grade students were investigated over a period of eight months.

Major conclusions reached were that the integrated distributive computer network system was more effective than traditional instruction in increasing reading, math and language achievement for low achieving students. It was as effective as traditional instruction in increasing achievement for high achieving students. It has had positive effects on student motivation, attitude, instructional task persistance, and the organisation, quantity and quality of student writing.

Schram (1965) reviewed 393 studies, comparing educational or instructional television with conventional classroom teaching in schools and colleges and came out with the following generalisations.

(i) Television has been used with greatest success in lower grades than in high schools or colleges.

(ii) Television instruction appears to have been most successful in mathematics, science and social studies and less successful in history, humanities and literature.

(iii) Attitude of college students towards televised instruction is less favourable than that of high school students.

(iv) There appears to be more resistance to television teaching at the college level than at the school level.

Smart-Leathy Ann (1994) studied the "effect of traditional versus multimedia augmented instruction on exposure time determination". The main purpose of this study was to compare the effectiveness of traditional instruction and traditional instruction augmented by a multimedia module for psychomotor learning and to determine if academic level and previous experience had an effect on accuracy of density determination for photographic print.

The experimental group that received the multimedia augmented lesson treatment had less absolute density error that is, the treatment had a positive effect.

Smith, Bonie Jean (1993) conducted a study on "implementation of satellite distance learning in Illinois rural secondary schools: A descriptive study". The purpose of the study was to provide an overview of the status of the WIU/ISBE, Satellite Network and use of the TI-IN Network satellite-delivered courses in rural and small schools in Illinois .and to determine the factors which contribute to a hospitable environment for the implementation of distance learning technology.

The results indicated that the satellite delivery of advanced courses is a recognised, accepted, utilized and beneficial approach to providing equal access to educational opportunities to secondary students in rural and small schools in Illinois. Like any other instructional innovation, the integration of interactive television technology into the existing school system demands the attention, care and planning of an effective administrator. The administrator needs to possess the leadership characteristics that not only allow a vision of what the educational technology offers the students and the school district, but also that provide the capabilities to effectively lead the implementation process.

Steele, Jerry Reed (1994) studied "bridging distances to the individual learner: The converging of video, voice and data technologies". The study concluded that examination and faculty experiences confirm that experimental group students performed better than students in traditional classrooms; formal delivery models force improved course organisation and preparation; on-going two-way interactivity encourages better student preparation, participation, and self assessment.

Tay, Young-Wu (1993) made "an assessment of the developmental status of educational technology in the People's Republic of China". Educational technology is a process for analysing problem in human learning and managing their solutions. This study subtly points out how vigorous efforts at promoting the application of educational technology have led to the establishment of central agencies at national levels, audio-visual education stations in rural areas, audio- visual centres in universities, and the operation of central and local radio and television universities.

Tenyankarn Me Donald (1994) made a study on "learner controlled lessons in co-operative learning groups during computer based instruction". This study investigated the effects of studying alone or in co-operative learning groups on the performance of high and low achievers. The study also examined the effects of computer based instruction using either learner or programme control.

This study concluded that both high and low achievers in the co-operative treatment increased achievement on programme controlled and learner controlled computer lessons. The learner controlled co-operative learning group made more options while checking their concept learning, and spent more time interacting with the learner controlled computer based tutorial, than the learner controlled individual learning group.

Winter, Christina Surrency (1994) devised "a strategy for identifying when interventions should occur in computer assisted instruction". The main purpose of the study was to develop, describe and demonstrate a system for assessing the normative or expected progress of pupils who are engaged in learning through computer-assisted instruction. A model is built which would enable an instructor to intervene as needed in the students' learning, thus encouraging early intervention of pending learning problems.

The 'learners' rates of progress were analysed by using the Markov method. By analysing the normative passage rate of the control group, a model of intervention was developed and demonstrated on an application group A Table of Probabilities and other tables generated by the Markov method, provided the basis for development of the intervention model and assessment of the computer assisted instruction.

Yorke (1977) sought to compare the relative effectiveness of the two short courses in the general methodology of teaching on the subsequent classroom performance of student teachers'. One course was wholly lecture based, while the other required students to develop their teaching competence through television lessons and teaching them to groups of approximately fifteen top junior pupils. These lessons were video recorded and the video recordings were discussed in the presence of a supervisor, who guided the discussion towards matters covered during the lecture course. The relativeness of the two treatments was assessed by comparing the subsequent classroom teaching performance of seven volunteer students from each group, the criterion being the performance of their pupils on a test constructed by the author. No significant difference was found between the two groups.

Critique of the Studies Under this Sub-head

It is important to note that some theoretical sources from other countries are not available in India. They reach us after some years. Most of the studies are referred to either in books or in Dissertation Abstracts International. The lack of adequate opportunity to peruse the original version of the foreign researchers adds hurdles in providing critique. However, an attempt is made to present critique based on the abstracts of the studies feted in this section.

Most of the studies are related to high technology instructional media (HTIM). They can be classified as studies related to video, TV and multimedia. The studies related to video attempt to establish the impact of video instruction on achievement of students. Use of video technology ensures better acquisition of knowledge and it is more effective to low ability group (Borras, 1993; Leitner, 1992; Schram, 1965; Steel, 1994). At the same time Naggy (1992) points out that the teachers in a typical school setting may not have the amount of time and expertise required for development of interactive video packages.

Studies on educational TV programmes bring to light contradictory findings. It is very effective in creating interest in preschool children (Lee, 1970). Only a few teachers use this medium effectively for dass viewing and mass viewing of programmes (Chotan *et al.*, 1986). Influence of television on children's leisure, interest, knowledge, outlook and values is much less colourful than it is expected (Himmelwett *et al.*, 1958) On the other hand, Foxall and Tom (1972) report positive influence of closed circuit television in training for teaching in Further Education Institution.

Quite a number of impressive studies have been undertaken to assess the impact of computer assisted instruction. Math computer assisted instruction has had positive impact on achievement of third and fourth grade students with mild teaming/behaviour disabilities (Dobbins, 1994). Computer modules have been verified to be effective as viable instructional aids (Elmore, 1992). Effectiveness of computer assisted instruction has been established in teaching science, reading, and math (Nishho, 1994; Schmidt, 1991). It has been found to be effective in increasing reading, math and language achievement of low achieving students (Schmidt, 1991). It envisages that more studies are to be attempted with special reference to backward children. Smart (1994) and Postlethwat (1964) have brought to light the impact of multimedia instructional strategy and its advantage over traditional method.

Studies Conducted Abroad on Modular Approach in Education

Studies conducted abroad on effectiveness of modular approach are presented under this sub-head.

Goldschmid and Goldschmid (1973) conducted an experimental study on "modular instruction in higher education' and proved that modular instruction turned out to be effective.

James W. Brown, Richard, Lewis, Fred (1985) state that the commercially produced learning centre modules play prominent roles in individualised learning and independent study. Commercially produced modules are now available for nearly all the subjects in curriculum. They also emphasise that these modules are more effective and economical. The Centre for Vocational Education of Ohio Sate University made a study on "present information with the chalk board and film chart module c29" and found that the presentation of the instructional materials in the form of modules was found to be more effective than the traditional presentation of instruction.

Russel, James, *et al.*, (1981) made a study on "improving competence through modular instruction".' Their study revealed that the modular instruction improved the competence of the students in a more effective manner than the traditional instructions. Also, the study revealed that the modular instruction ensured mastery level learning at the learners' own pace.

Studies Conducted Abroad on Low Achievement/ Slow Learner

Quite a number of studies have been conducted abroad with regard to backward children, learning disabled, low achievers and slow learners. Here, some studies related to slow learners and low achievers are summed up under this sub-heading.

Allington and Johnston (1986) Brantlinger and Guskin (1987), Brophy (1986) Jenkins (1987) have reported considerable similarity in the behavioural characteristics of the two groups, viz, the students with mild disabilities and the economically disadvantaged students who often constitute low achievers, including low achievement, inefficient learning difficulties in correlated processes such as visual and auditory perception and social/behavioural difficulties.

Bob Lumpkins *et al.,* (1991) conducted an experimental study on effectiveness of "instructional equity for low achievers in elementary school mathematics". The major purpose of this study was to test the effect of an innovative programme designed to help low-achieving fourth and fifth grade students to increase their achievement in mathematics. Attention was also given to the effect of this programme on other achievers to determine whether their achievement would be positively or negatively affected.

The findings of the study clearly suggest the conclusion that this programme was effective with both low and normal achievers. Factors such as the grouping strategies, lesson plan designs, extended class period for mathematics, instructional methodologies and teacher expectations may have contributed either or in combination, to the achievement gains.

Burt (1946) states that one of the most frequent complaints about backward children is the weakness of their memory. Of all the special disabilities that hamper educational progress, the most frequent is a weakness in what may be termed long distance memory. Dull children seem to need to go over the material more times before it is fixed in their minds and more frequent revision is required to prevent forgetting.

Cartner and Lipskey (1987), Jenkins, Pious and Peterson (1988) report only equivocal results regarding the differences between the students with mild disability and low achieving students. A particular subject of much controversy and debate is the apparent lack of any major differences in education-related characteristics or outcomes for students classified as learning disabled and students with low academic achievements.

Cleugh., M.F. (1957) points out that the wide ESN umbrella is in danger of being misused to provide a haven for pupils who should have been provided for in other ways. Pupils like slow learners, who are generally not mentally retarded, could be provided for in ordinary schools where adequate facilities are widely available. There must be some comprehensive provision for a special educational treatment in such ordinary school. Meanwhile, there is a danger that some children whose limited capacities really merit the support and the preparation for living given in the ESN school may be overlooked, while others whose immediate difficulties call attention to them are being admitted to ESN schools.

Conner (1983) Gresham and Reschly (1986) have found large differences between the students classified as mildly disabled and the students with average levels of performance.

Conner (1983) Damberg (1983) Prooks and McCauley (1984), Hallahan and Sappona (1984), in addition to differences in achievement, have reported specific differences between the two groups of learning disabled and low achievers in a variety of information processing variables, including efficiency of learning, prior knowledge, information processing strategies and meta cognitive operation for directing the learning process.

Duncan, J. (1942)—believed that higher performance quotients showed that the sub-normal children should be taught by methods based on thinking and problem solving in practical activities. The low attainment of slow learners is due to an educational approach through the medium of words, their weakest factor. He laid stress on practical activities and concrete experiences. A special attack on language backwardness of sub normal children is required, both indirectly through the concrete and practical and directly through the medium of language and verbal experiences.

Oliver, J.N. (1956) compared growth of 100 ESN boys with 100 normal boys graphing their growth on the Wetzel Grid. The results showed that there were more smaller boys among the ESN group. 57 ESN boys and 36 normal boys were below the standard growth line. There were more deviations from normal growth among the ESN boys. Oliver concludes from an examination of the literature in the subject that the all-round fitness of the ESN tends to be below par compared with that of normal children and that this is likely to lead to fatigue, general muscular debility and postural defects.

Peterson (1989) in his study "Remediation is no Remedy" found that the academic performance of low achievers is improved when they are instructed in a group that includes high achievers. If instructional grouping is felt to be necessary when the students differ significantly in achievement, educators need to find ways to lessen the negative effect on low achievers.

Pringle and Bassio (1958), Sarason (1948) administered Wechsler Scales to sub normal children and found their verbal quotients to be lower. They suggested that this lower verbal quotients may be due to the sub normal child's emotional response to a face to face interview in which oral replies are required. In such an interview, emotional factors resulting from the child's previous experiences of failure in school and in interpersonal situations might be expected to inhibit verbalisation. It is indeed noticeable how some children turn with relief from verbal to practical tests.

Ross (1977) in his book entitled "Psychological aspects of Learning Disabilities and Reading Disorders" outlined clearly in what way the learning disabled are different from the mentally retarded, the physically handicapped, the emotionally disturbed and the culturally disadvantaged.

A learning disabled child is not mentally retarded. He is a child whose intellectual capacity is below the normal range. His or her difficulty almost always affects every area of behaviour which involves learning. Such a child would have been late in acquisition of language, slow in learning certain motor skills. In school, such a child will have trouble in all subject areas, be it writing, spelling, reading or arithmetic.

Runyan (1991) examined the reading comprehension performance of learning disabled and non-learning disabled college and university students under timed and untimed conditions. The major findings of the study were:

(i) There is a significant difference between scores obtained by students with learning disabilities and the non-LD students under timed conditions.

(ii) LD students significantly improved their scores with extra time, while non-LD students in both high and low-achieving groups, did not.

(iii) High-achieving LD students made greater gains in improvement than low-achieving LD students when given extra time.

Tansley and Gulliford (1962) remark that one of the causes of poor memory in slow learners is weakness in attention. What is to be learned must be attended to and its main features observed. Failure in this may be due to factors in the child such as restlessness and distractibility. Also, attention may be poor because the material to be learned is unsuitable—too difficult or outside the child's experience. It may be that it is presented in a way that does not facilitate accurate perceptions of it.

Teel (1994) assessed "low achievement" among inner-city African American middle school students. It was a teacher-researcher's classroom study. The purpose of the study was to assess the issues of low self-esteem, negative motivation, and poor academic achievement through a culturally and academically sensitive classroom approach for junior high school African-American history students at risk of school failure. A key component of this study was assessment of the impact of this approach on the students attitudes, behaviour and performance.

Findings: After two years of classroom research, using a relatively non-traditional teaching approach with "low-achieving" African-American students, the investigator found that students at risk of school failure can become just as engaged and motivated as students identified as "high achievers". Given a non-competitive, supportive classroom environment the majority of students demonstrated improvements in overall effort, in their speaking and writing skills and in their confidence in themselves as students.

A series of researches over a period of four years conducted at the University of Okalahoma (1952) showed that an over achiever is characteristically more self aware and willing to take responsibility. On the other hand an under achiever is guided by mutually contradictory motives and is not aware of his conflicting nature. The investigator concluded that intellectual variables can function effectively only when the personality function is properly integrated.

Weitz, Clerk and Jones (1955) have reported the definiteness of optional choice of the major field of study to be significantly related to over and under achievement In each of these studies, the over achieving group tended to have more definite plans than did their underachieving counterparts.

Willot's (1953) study on secondary school slow learning children revealed the importance of orientation, family background, adoption to studies and particularly the method of teaching for their academic success.

Critique of the Studies under this Sub-head

As there is no internet facility either in his university where he carried out the research work, or in his school where he actually conducted the experiment, the investigator experienced considerable difficulty in getting access to important theoretical sources. All that he could do was to depend on Dissertation. Abstracts International and other books for review of foreign studies. These books seldom provide us with adequate information required for attempting to engage with their relative strengths and weaknesses in respect to the conceptualisations and theoretical contributions. So the studies under this sub-head have been reported without critique. However an attempt is made now to connect and contrast studies.

There are considerable similarities between learning disabled students and low achieving students. Also, no significant difference is found in education related characteristics or outcomes between learning disabled students and low achieving students (Allington and Johnson, 1986; Cartner and Lipskey, 1987). Some other studics point out there are marked differences between learning disabled students and low achieving students in a variety of information processing variables, including efficiency of learning, prior knowledge, information processing strategies, and meta cognitive operation (Conner, 1983; Damberg, 1984; Hallahan and Sappona, 1984;).

Peterson (1989) stresses that academic performance of low achievers can be enhanced when they are instructed in a group that includes high achievers. Similarly, Bab Lumpkins *et al.*, (1991) report that their innovative programme designed to help low achieving fourth and fifth grade students to increase their achievement in mathematics has been effective with both low and normal achievers. These two above studies tend a give theoretical support to the inclusive education concept of Mel Ainscow (1997, 1998). This emphasises the need to design specific instructional strategy that can reach out to all learners.

AN OVERVIEW OF THE RESEARCHES REVIEWED

A critical review of the studies covered in this chapter reveals that most of the studies have been conducted for measuring the effectiveness of LTIM and HTIM. A glimpse of researches on educational technology done in India discloses that most of the studies on media and technology have been conducted in formal education situations. Generally researches on instructional media in India have had the following foci: developing materials, establishing effectiveness of materials, learners' and teachers' attitude towards media, media usability and cost-effectiveness. Most of the studies concentrate on conventional school system.

Instructional media studies can be classified under four areas viz.:

(i) Print based written texts like Programmed Learning Material, Modular Approach, Open Learning Material, etc.,

(ii) Audio-Visual aids including both LTIM and HTIM where all the low cost teaching aids come under LTIM and radio, TV, audio and video cassettes etc., come under HTIM,

(iii) Computer Assisted Instruction, and

(iv) Multimedia Instructional Packages. Most of the studies conducted on above areas have focussed on the following:

   (i) development of instructional materials;

   (ii) Effectiveness of materials/media from the point of view of achievement of instructional objectives, comparability with other materials/media, and other criteria;

   (iii) attitude of learners; user teachers and others concerned with instructional system towards media;

   (iv) usability of media, cost effectiveness, time management etc.

George (1966) Golani (1982), Sastri (1982) have proved the effectiveness of audio visual aids on the achievement of students.

They also pointed out that most of the teachers don't prefer to use audio-visual aids because of heavy cost, heavy syllabus, insufficient number of material aids and lack of skill and special training. At the same times Edward Sahaya Raj (1994) Shah and Gupta (1986) point out how it is possible to develop low cost teaching aids and how they are cost effective and time effective besides being effective in achieving the educational objectives.

The experimental studies on radio broadcast programmes are of three types: pre-test and post-test study of direct broadcast programmes in natural setting (Singh and Shukla, 1980); introducing radio vision method of teaching in comparison to traditional method (Oberai, 1985 and Dhamija, 1985); and developing systematic strategies for using School Broadcast Programme (SBP) with pre broadcast, during broadcast with visual supplement and post broadcast activities (Biswal, 1982; Sudame *et al.*, 1988). In the case of all kinds of experimental studies, results go in favour of radio instruction inputs in terms of gain of achievement scores as well as appreciation by teachers and students. Studies conducted on self instructional audio cassettes by (Kour, 1981; Kumar, 1981; Ramar, 1994) reveal that self instructional audio cassettes are effective in developing different skills.

As for TV and Video, quite a number of studies have been conducted in India as well as abroad. One can witness a number of studies on Educational Television (ETV) programmes at different levels, such as: formal school stage, formal higher education stage, open university stage, and functional literacy/ extension education stage. Such studies can be categorised under two headings, viz., utilisation studies and effectiveness studies.

Studies on utilisation of general enrichment as well as course based ETV programmes at school and college levels in India indicate a poor picture. Major reasons identified for poor utilisation of ETV at school level are linked with institutional Time Table, management and availability of physical facilities, lack of awareness and initiative by teachers and institutional authorities; lack of co-ordination between programme co-ordinating bodies and schools; placement and maintenance of T.V. sets etc.; poor power supply; dubbing programmes in different languages etc (Holtzman and Isabel, 1981; Phutela, 1980; Reddy Usha and Vyasula, 1985; Singhal *et al.*, 1988).

Experimental studies on effectiveness of ETV are of four types viz., effectiveness of ETV with pre-test and post-test design; effectiveness of ETV with additional input of interaction among peers and the expert teachers in classroom setting; effectiveness of ETV with additional input facilities for interaction of student viewers with the experts available at central telecast station through two way audio and one way video exposures; and production and validation of local level video programmes.

Experimental studies on ETV conducted at school and college levels indicate favourable results in term of viewers' language development (Kanade, 1982; seth 1983); general academic performance; and gain scores in subject areas (Phutela, 1980; Doneriya, 1988; Jaiswal, 1988; and Hiaman and Purushottaman, 1991). Studies on video have established the effectiveness of video instruction in terms of achievement, cost and benefit. (Hiaman and Purushothaman, 1988; Jayalakshmi, 1982; Kalimuthu, 1991; Karpaga Kumaravel, 1988, Sinnathambi, 1991; Mallick and Sahoo, 1994; Steele, 1994; Borras Isabel, 1994; Naggy, 1992; Leitner, 1992).

Though not in large number as in occidental countries, some studies have been undertaken in India on computer application and on effectiveness of computer assisted instruction. In India it is a budding area of research in educational technology. The major focus of the studies on computer assisted instruction has been on:

(i) development of CAI software for different subjects at school and college stages;

(ii) studying their effectiveness in terms of achievement, teachers' and students' reactions towards CAI;

(iii) comparisons of CAI with traditional method of teaching; and

(iv) uses of computers in different areas like daily teaching, management of education, library, examination and guidance activities.

All studies conducted on effectiveness of CAI indicate favourable results in terms of achievement of instructional objectives. Moreover, the CAI materials have been found to be superior to traditional mode of teaching. In all cases, greater learning gains have been evinced (Stella, 1993; Mahajan, 1992; Elmore, 1992; Robert, 1994; Schmidt, 1992; Benaloh, 1994; Nishino, 1994).

Albeit on a lesser scale, adequate number of studies have been conducted on modular approach both in India and abroad. It has been confirmed that modules are effective with regard to achievement of cognitive objectives mostly at knowledge, understanding and application levels as well as development of certain teaching skills. Immediate gain and retention of newly acquired informations have been found upto expected level among students using modules. The modular approach has been found very effective in the case of school level as well as at college level subjects covering different areas such as science, mathematics, languages, social sciences, home science etc (Dhamija, 1985; Gabriel, Pillai and Gnanam, 1989; Jayalakshmi, 1985; Sahajahan, 1980; Hopper, 1982; Ramar, 1994; Reddy and Ramar, 1994,1995,1996; James Russel *et al.*, 1981;) The modules have been found effective not only in printed forms but also in the forms of softwares of audio lessons, video lessons and computer assisted instruction (Subramania Pillai, 1992; Ramar, 1994; Reddy and Ramar 1994, 1995, 1996).

Coming to low achievement and slow learning, adequate number of studies have been conducted on low achievers both in India and abroad whereas quite a few studies have been conducted specifically on slow learners. Most of the studies have been done to analyse the causes and factors of low achievement and personality variables of low achievers (Deka, 1985; Koul, 1978; Saun, 1980; Singh, 1983; Singh, 1986; Somasundaram, 1980; Peterson, 1989; Teel, 1994). Some studies have been undertaken to assess the effectiveness of different instructional strategies on the achievement of low achievers (Ramar, 1994; Reddy and Ramar, 1994, 1995, 1996; Janakkumar 1996, Block and Burns, 1976; Bloom, 1976, 1984; Slavin, 1986).

Adequate studies on slow learners are not available. Only a very few studies have been conducted so far. Most of books on slow learning written by Coleman *et al.*, (1966), Tansley and Gulliford (1962), Beasley (1956), Ingram (1953) Cleugh, 1957; Kirk (1940, 1962, 1972) and Jenson (1980) highlight the causes of slow learning and the personality factors of slow learners and also they suggest ways and means to surmount slow learning. But experimental studies on slow learners are found inadequate. Soundararaja Rao and Rajaguru (1995) have assessed the effectiveness of video instruction on the achievement of slow learners.

From the reviews done, it is interesting to note that there is no clear cut demarcation between the low achievers and the slow learners. There are many common characteristics and qualities. While the students who get fail scores in all the subjects are low achievers, such students who score less than 25 per cent in all the subjects may be termed as slow learners. All the slow learners are usually low achievers. This may, perhaps, be the reason why many researchers prefer to use the broad spectrum term "low achiever' and so studies on slow learners are found in meagre number.

The review of related research reveals that various studies have brought to light the effectiveness of different components of multimedia based modular approach on the achievement of students in general. Only a few studies on effectiveness of multimedia based modular approach have been conducted with special reference to low achievers. But, sufficient studies have not been undertaken with special reference to slow learners who constitute about 18 per cent of the student population. So more studies to measure the effectiveness of media applications with special reference to slow learners are warranted.

Moreover, we are passing through an era of auto instruction and improved educational technology. To keep pace with the developed countries we have to accentuate the human resource development to a great extent and, that too, at the earliest possible time. This envisages special instructional strategies to boost up the performance of backward students like low achievers and slow learners. Since auto instruction is the trend of the time, it will be very much in the interest of student population to undertake more researches on media application with special reference tc slow learners. The present study is an earnest attempt to develop multimedia based modules and to measure their effectiveness with special reference to slow learners.

The statement of the problem of the study is presented in the next chapter.

3

STATEMENT OF THE PROBLEM

This chapter is confined to the title of the problem, objectives, hypotheses, scope, need and importance and limitations of the study.

TITLE OF THE PROBLEM

"EFFECTIVENESS OF MULTIMEDIA BASED MODULAR APPROACH WITH SPECIAL REFERENCE TO SLOW LEARNERS"

MEANING OF CERTAIN TERMS USED IN THE STUDY

Under this sub-head the meaning and definition of the key terms used in the study along with the operational definition of the investigator are listed out.

Effectiveness

According to Oxford Dictionary (1975) effectiveness is 'being able to bring about the result intended'.

Champers Twentieth Century Dictionary (1972) defines effectiveness as—'being successful in producing a result or effect'.

As far as this study is concerned effectiveness refers to the impressive result produced in the learning of slow learners consequent to the operation of multimedia based modules.

Effectiveness refers to the degree of realisation of educational objectives. It also refers to the degree of realisation of higher level attainment.

Module

Subramania Pillai (1992) defines module as "a self contained and self instructional package dealing with a single conceptual unit or subject matter."

James Brown *et al.*, (1985) define modules as "the correlated units or packages of instructional materials which play prominent roles in individualised learning and independent study."

In this study, module is a self contained, suitably tested auto-instructional material. It is a learning package which contains everything needed by the student for self instruction.

Multimedia

Chambers Twentieth Century Dictionary (1972) defines multimedia as "simultaneous presentation in one place of several visual and/or sound entertainments".

According to Turner (1985) multimedia refers to "transmitting of information to the pupils through audio and video devices rather than hierarchically from the teacher."

Dipika B. Shah (1988) defines multimedia as "more than one medium used in a single communication either sequentially or simultaneously."

According to Encyclopedia of Education "multimedia instructional system" refers to the use of appropriate and carefully selected varieties of learning experiences which, when presented to the learner through selected teaching strategies, reinforce and strengthen one another so that the learner will achieve predetermined and desired behavioural objectives.

In this study, multimedia refers to transmitting of information to the pupils through more than one medium in a single communication either sequentially or simultaneously. Multimedia means making appeal to different senses instead of one as in the traditional method. Multimedia instructional strategy refers to the instructional strategy which incorporates minimum two or more than two media in its instructional process so as to enable the pupils to achieve predetermined and desired behavioural objectives. In this study multimedia refers to the use of judicious blend of appropriate media to teach the specified units of the subjects. The following factors were the criteria for selection of appropriate media to teach the instructional units in this study:

Task factors

Learner factors

Physical attributes

Economic factors and Instructional factors.

The nature of the task undertaken, the nature of the subject earmarked for experiment, the requirements of the learners for better acquisition of informations and the feasibility and effectiveness of media in imparting informations played a decisive role in selection of appropriate media for inclusion in the multimedia approach of this study.

In this study, multimedia includes High Technology Instructional Media (HTIM) as well as Low Technology Instructional Media (LTIM). Under HTIM it includes audio and video cassettes procured from the International Educational Research Centre, New Delhi and also projector, microscope, slides, etc., available in the school. Under LTIM it includes globes, charts, pictures and other A.V. aids prepared making use of the resources locally available.

Slow Learners

While describing educationally subnormal children, the famous educational psychologist Gulliford perceives two broad distinctions—one group of children who by nature have limited intellectual endowment are depressed and there are others whose ability is not quite so limited but who nevertheless have more difficulty in learning than average children. While the former group is termed as "Slow Learners" the latter group is called under achievers (Soundara Raja Rao and Rajaguru, 1995).

Burt (1946) defines slow learners as those students who are unable to cope with the work normally expected of their age group.

According to Ramakrishnaiah and Shivappa (1995) a slow learner is one who is unable to do the work of the class in which he is placed or even the class below that. He does not respond satisfactorily to the ordinary school curriculum and to the usual methods and procedures of the classroom teaching. He is not upto the attainment levels of the various subjects which are normal for his age or grade.

Students with IQ 80 to 90, who are traditionally labelled "dull normal" are generally slower to 'catch on' to whatever is being taught if it involves symbolic, abstract or conceptual subject matter. In the early grades in school, they most often have problems in reading and arithmetic and are labelled "slow learners". But it is really not that they learn so slowly as that they lag behind in developmental readiness to grasp the concepts that are within easy reach of the majority of their age mates. Such children will eventually grasp these basic concepts or subjects fairly easily but about a year or two later than their age mates (Jensen, 1980). So they may be called rather "slow developers" than "slow learners".

In this study slow learners are those students whose learning rate is low and who lag behind in academic achievement always scoring fail marks, especially below 25 per cent in the test. They are the students who are unable to keep up with their age mates in academic achievement. Also, they are not up to the attainment levels in various subjects which are normal for his age or grade. They are found weak in almost all the subjects. They remain in the lowest rung of the ladder. They are the students who have to stagger and struggle even for a pass score.

OBJECTIVES OF THE STUDY

The following are the objectives of the study.

(1) To develop multimedia based modules for English, maths, science, and social science subjects of Std VIII.

(2) To assess the achievement of slow learners in Std VIII. when the subjects are taught through traditional lecture wethod.

(3) To find out achievement of slow learners in Std VIII when the subjects are taught through multimedia based modular approach.

(4) To find out the achievement of normal students in Std VIII when the subjects are taught through traditional lecture method.

(5) To find out whether there exists any significant difference between the pre-test mean scores of the control group slow learners and experimental group slow learners.

(6) To assess whether there exists any significant difference between the pre-test mean scores of control group slow learners and the normal group students.

(7) To find out whether there is any significant difference between the pre-test mean scores of experimental group slow learners and the normal group students.

(8) To assess whether there exists any significant difference between the pre-test and post-test mean scores of control group slow learners when the subjects are taught through traditional lecture method.

(9) To find out whether there is any significant difference between the pre-test and post-test mean scores of experimental group slow learners when the subjects are taught through multimedia based modular approach.

(10) To assess whether there exists any significant difference between the pre-test and post-test mean scores of normal group students taught through traditional lecture method.

(11) To find out whether there is any significant difference between the post-test mean scores of the slower learners in the experimental group and the slow learners in the control group.

(12) To assess whether there exists any significant difference between the post-test mean scores of the slow learning boys and the slow learning girls in the control group taught through traditional lecture method.

(13) To find out whether there is any significant difference between the post-test mean scores of the slow learning boys and the slow learning girls in the experimental group taught through multimedia based modular approach.

(14) To assess whether there exists any significant difference between the post-test mean scores of the slow learners in the control group and the students in the normal group.

(15) To find out whether there is any significant difference between the post-test mean scores of the slow learners in the experimental group and the students in the normal group.

(16) To assess whether there exists any significant difference between the post-test and retention test mean scores of the control group slow learners.

(17) To find out whether there is any significant difference between the post-test and retention test mean scores of the slow learners in the experimental group.

(18) To assess whether there exists any significant difference between the post-test and retention test mean scores of normal group students.

(19) To assess whether there exists any significant difference between the retention test mean scores of the slow learning boys and slow learning girls in the control group.

(20) To find out whether there is any significant difference between the retention test mean scores of the slow learning boys and the slow learning girls in the experimental group.

(21) To assess whether there exists any significant difference between the pre-test and post-test mean scores of the experimental group slow learners in English subject.

(22) To find out whether there is any significant difference between the pre-test and post-test mean scores of the experimental group slow learners in mathematics subject.

(23) To assess whether there is any significant difference between the pre-test and post-test mean scores of the experimental group slow learners in science subject.

(24) To find out whether there is any significant difference between the pre-test and post-test mean scores of the experimental group slow learners in social science subject.

(25) To assess whether the relative effectiveness of multimedia modular approach differs from subject to subject selected for this study.

ASSUMPTIONS OF THE STUDY

(1) Multimedia based modules can be developed for all the subjects in Standard VIII.

(2) Multimedia based modular approach is more effective than the traditional lecture method.

(3) Multimedia based modular approach enables the students in general, to score higher marks.

(4) Multimedia based modular approach enables the slow learners, in particular, to score higher marks.

(5) Multimedia based modular approach enables the slow learners to narrow down the gap between them and the normal students.

(6) The slow learners evince a favourable attitude towards multimedia based modular approach.

HYPOTHESES OF THE STUDY

Keeping in view the objectives of the study, the following hypotheses are formulated for testing:

(1) There exists no significant difference between the pre-test mean scores of control group slow learners and experimental group slow learners.

(2) There exists significant difference between the pre-test mean scores of control group slow learners and the normal group students.

(3) There exists significant difference between the pre-test mean scores of experimental group slow learners and the normal group students.

(4) There exists no significant difference between the pre-test and post-test mean scores of control group slow learners when the subjects are taught through traditional lecture method.

(5) There exists significant difference between the pre-test and post-test mean scores of experimental group slow learners taught through multimedia based modular approach.

(6) There exists no significant difference between the pre-test and post-test mean scores of normal group students taught through traditional lecture method.

(7) There exists significant difference between the post-test mean scores of the slow learners in the experimental group and the slow learners in the control group.

(8) There exists significant difference between the post-test mean scores of the slow learning boys and slow learning girls in the control group.

(9) There is significant difference between the post-test mean scores of the slow learning boys and slow learning girls in the experimental group.

(10) There exists significant difference between the post-test mean scores of the slow learners in the control group and the students in the normal group.

(11) There exists no significant difference between the post-test mean scores of the slow learners in the experimental group and the students in the normal group.

(12) There is no significant difference between the post-test and retention test mean scores of the control group slow learners.

(13) There exists no significant difference between the post-test and retention test mean scores of the slow learners in the experimental group.

(14) There is no significant difference between the post-test and retention test mean scores of normal group students.

(15) There exists significant difference between the retention test mean scores of the slow learning boys and the slow learning girls in the control group.

(16) There exists significant difference between the retention test mean scores of the slow learning boys and slow learning girls in the experimental group.

(17) There exists significant difference between the pre-test and post-test mean scores of the experimental group slow learners in English subject.

(18) There exists significant difference between the pre-test and post-test mean scores of the experimental group slow learners in mathematics subject.

(19) There exists significant difference between the pre-test and post-test mean scores of the experimental group slow learners in science subject.

(20) There exists significant difference between the pre-test and post-test mean scores of the experimental group slow learners in social science subject.

(21) Relative effectiveness of multimedia based modular approach differs from subject to subject.

SCOPE OF THE STUDY

Multimedia is a composite of auditory and visual presentation. It can reach an audience of unlimited size. It can transmit programme content without delay from the point of origin to the point of reception. Keeping this view in mind, the primary focus of the study is to develop multimedia based modules for certain units in all the subjects of standard VIII, except Tamil. Four main constituents of multimedia are used in this study. They are:

(1) Audio Cassettes

(2) Video Cassettes

(3) Software for computer assisted instruction.

(4) Other HTIM and LTIM available in the school.

Audio cassettes procured from the International Educational Research Centre, New Delhi, and ACE Educational Systems Pvt. Ltd., Madras, which cover most of the units, are used in this study in addition to the audio cassettes developed by the researcher covering the left out units. The instructional presentation by the teacher was recorded so as to suit the slow learners.

Likewise, the video cassettes procured from the International Educational Research Centre, New Delhi were used to provide multimedia base to the modules relevant to the particular concepts. For those units for which ready made cassettes were not available, required multimedia packages were developed by the investigator himself.

In addition to the audio and video cassettes, computer software for computer assisted instruction was also prepared. The computer assisted instruction was programmed in such a way as to promote auto learning by the slow learner at his own pace. These multimedia packages were developed with the help of concerned technical experts and subject resource persons.

Apart from the audio and video cassettes procured from different agencies and developed by the investigator, other HTIM like microscope, microslides etc., and LTIM such as colour charts, models both working and non working etc., were also used as an integral part of multimedia based modules.

Modules of all the units were given to the experimental group slow learners in the form of a Handbook so as to facilitate auto learning by the slow learners at their own pace. Teacher support system was limited to the extent of operating the multimedia packages, clarifying doubts and guiding the project works.

Three units were selected for each subject for the purpose of developing and measuring the effectiveness of multimedia based modules. Each unit was divided into two to four conceptual sub-units. For mathematics equations, inequations, circular ring, cube and cuboid were selected for the study. For science one unit from physics *i.e.*, magnetism, one unit from chemistry *i.e.*, compounds of carbon and another unit from biology *i.e.*, cellular organisations were included in the study. For social science subject one unit from history *i.e.*, religious and social reformations, one unit from civics *i.e.*, defence organisations in India and one more unit from geography *i.e.*, Indian forests and wild life were selected for study. For English, since language plays a more prominent role than the subject matter, sentence pattern and non-finite verbs and spoken English covering pure vowels, diphthongs and consonants were earmarked for preparation of modules.

Fifty slow learners of S.S.H.N. Higher Secondary School, Muhavoor were selected for the study. Twenty five of them constituted the experimental group while the rest formed the control group. The main focus of the study is to measure the effectiveness and advantage of multimedia based modular approach over the traditional lecture method in promoting the achievement of the slow learners in standard VIII. In addition to the pre-test and post-test, a retention test was also conducted to assess the impact of multimedia based modular approach on the retention of the slow learners. Finally, the study also aims to measure the extent to which the multimedia based modular approach enables the slow learners to cope with normal students. For this purpose, a normal group was also constituted comprising twenty five average and above average students selected from the population, from which the sample for the study was drawn.

NEED AND IMPORTANCE OF THE STUDY

Teaching effectively is the most important of all the competencies required of a successful teacher. Since effective teaching deals with the needs, interest and abilities of pupils as individuals, it requires knowledge of the environment in which the pupil lives, the development problem he or she faces and his/her mental abilities. It is more true so when the teacher is dealing with the slow learners. It also calls for an understanding of the learning processes essential for creating an environment where learning can take place and for making instruction so stimulating that every pupil will be motivated to learn. Stimulating pupils to think critically, independently and creatively is essential for effective teaching.

Effective teaching in any subject depends largely upon the introduction of newer methods of instruction. There is a growing need for trying out newer methods of instruction and establishing their effectiveness in teaching. Now-a-days a teacher cannot depend on any single method of teaching. The teacher has to try out several innovative methods to present the content to the students. When they are taught by innovative methods, the students are able to understand the concept, principles and content in an effective manner.

The immense knowledge explosion taking place in the world warrants newer methods of teaching. Students need unique experience in the presentation of the content. Multimedia based modular approach provides such unique experience to students. But, utmost care should be evinced in development of modules and multimedia packages which is a complex technical work.

Destiny of a nation is being shaped in her classrooms. The growing number of slow learners at all levels of our educational system warrants such a study, as this proposed one, to be undertaken for the enrichment of our teaching learning process.

Above all, human resource development should be at the focus of any research effort for a developing country like India which has abundant human resources. In the Indian system of education, it is observed that the human resources-teachers and learners, are under developed and perform less than their capabilities. The learners are under developed in the sense that they are not achieving in tune with their capabilities. Even some of the most efficient teachers are not adequately equipped to identify and guide the under achievers and slow learners to reach their optimum levels. As a result, the institutions in turn are not able to send their products into the society as fully developed learners. To ensure this we need a different strategy which can cater to individual differences. Multimedia based modular approach is such a strategy.

Although, much has been achieved in this field of education, there are many opportunities for experiment and research. Throughout we have been constantly aware of the need for further investigation of the learning, thinking and adjustment of slow learning children so that teaching method can be precisely planned to suit their needs (Tansley and Gulliford, 1962).

Now, the current trend is propagating auto learning by the learner himself at his own pace. This paved the way for CAI, CAL, etc., Here the teacher is merely a facilitator of learning. He need not suffocate the learners with all the informations at a time. In auto learning, the learner can take his own time and he can proceed at his own pace till he completes the lesson. It is not the time but mastery learning which is the governing criterion here. This is where the multimedia based modular approach exactly fits in.

Multimedia learning experiences represent a natural way for learning to take place. Learning can be accelerated by involving maximum number of senses. Sensory experience forms the foundation of intellectual activity within any formal school situation and learners differ in the effectiveness of their sense reception. Multimedia learning experiences have the advantage of appealing to the individual, the learner's pace, interest and readiness.

Besides, cognition and conceptualisation depend on a chain of events which begin with the learner's perception of stimulus, be the auditory, visual, tactile and olfactory. It is important that these initial learning experiences be accurate, dependable and understandable. Unless the learner's initial sensory impressions are accurate, it will be impossible for them to have reliable conceptualisation and understandings. With the existing numerous kinds of aids, carefully organised presentation of information through a variety of media should occupy the learner's conscious attention to living stimuli (Mohan &

Rajeswari, 1995). This is what is precisely ensured by the multimedia based modular approach.

Multimedia based modules help to stimulate interest in learning. It economises time and effort, reduces verbalism in teaching and imparts broad education to pupils. Not only children but also adults remember facts better when the multimedia aids are used to explain the concepts. Further, multimedia based modular approach supports Paivio's (1971) dual code theory of memory which suggests that information coded both visually and verbally is remembered better than information coded in only one of those two ways.

Instructors sometimes consider it difficult or impossible to individualise learning while carrying on group instruction. But opportunities do exist to individualise learning with group of nearly any size (James Brown *et al.*, 1985). To do so requires systematic planning and creative uses of media sources as in modularisation.

Multimedia has come in to stay for ever to wield a greater influence in the teaching learning process. There is very urgent need to experiment the effectiveness of multimedia based modules and to assess their advantage over the traditional lecture method. In the Indian setting, studies have been made by Vardhini (1983), Krishnan (1983), Menon (1984) and Basu (1981) to prove the effectiveness of multimedia. Dhamija (1985) Hopper (1982) and Sahajahan (1980), Chelladurai (1994), Natarajan (1996) have conducted experimental studies to prove and measure the effectiveness of modular approach. Ramar (1994), Lokanadha Reddy and Ramar (1994, 1995, 1996) have conducted experimental studies to bring to light and to measure the effectiveness of multimedia based modular approach. But, no attempt has been made to study the effectiveness of multimedia based modular approach with special reference to slow learners.

Systematic researches are, therefore, necessary to develop multimedia based modules so as to assess their effectiveness with special reference to slow learners. Also, we cannot afford to ignore the slow learners who constitute a sizeable portion of student population. The present study is an attempt to develop multimedia based modules for the use of slow learners learning in Standard VIII and to measure their effectiveness with special reference to slow learners and also to assess their advantage over the traditional lecture method.

LIMITATIONS OF THE STUDY

The limitations of the study are as follows:

(1) This study is confined to the slow learners studying in standard VIII of S.S.H.N. Higher Secondary School, Muhavoor.

(2) The sample consists of only 50 slow learners selected on the basis of teachers observation, their performance in RPM and also on the basis of rate of learning.

(3) For all the chosen subjects, only three units each were included for the study.

(4) For English subject, only two units of language items and spoken English covering vowels, diphthongs and consonants were included in the experiment.

(5) The experiment was conducted for a period of 45 working days @ 1½ hours-per-day.

(6) Multimedia packages were developed based on the video shooting done in the classroom where the experiment was actually conducted by making use of the technical expertise available in the district HQ. It is to be noted that the institution where the experiment was conducted is located at a remote rural area far from the madding crowd.

(7) The achievement test used in the study is a teacher made one and not a standardised one. The methodology used in this study is presented in the forthcoming chapter.

4

METHODOLOGY

This chapter deals with the methodology followed in the study. The methodology followed in the study is discussed under different headings namely-development of modules to teach the subjects of class VIII syllabi, development of multimedia packages including software for CAI, identifying slow learners, teaching by multimedia based modular approach, construction of research tools, sampling techniques, design of the study, administration of tools for pre-test and post-test and retention test, statistical techniques employed for analysing the obtained data.

DEVELOPMENT OF MODULES

The major objective of this study is to prepare modules for all the subjects in Standard VIII. In the development of modules/ the guidelines given by the NCERT and the models of Subramania Pillai of Madurai Kamaraj University (1992) have been followed by the investigator. In English, since learning of English language is more important than learning the subject matter of prose and poetry, non-finite verbs, sentence patterns and vowels and consonants were chosen for the purpose of developing modules and experimentation. In maths, three units *i.e.*, equations and inequations, cube and cuboid and circular ring, in science, one unit from physics, *i.e.*, magnetism, one unit from chemistry *i.e.*, compounds of carbon and one unit from biology *i.e.*, cellular organisation were included in the study for developing multimedia based modules. In social science, one unit from history *i.e.,* religious and social reformations, one unit from civics *i.e.,* defence organisation in India and one unit from geography *i.e.,* Indian forests and wild life, were selected for the purpose of this study. Each of the above units was divided into three to four conceptual sub units. Each sub unit constituted the subject content for development of one module. Each module was developed in self-contained and self-instructional manner. Each has at its first page the overview of the module which specifies the unit, the conceptual sub-unit and the pattern of the module. Below the overview is given the list of multimedia packages available for the auto learning of the users.

In the succeeding page, instruction is given to the students as to how to use the module for self learning. The third page contains the entry test consisting of objective type test items to assess the preliminary knowledge or the entering levels of competence of the students required for learning the module. If a student fails to obtain the prescribed minimum level of competence or achievement, he may not understand the module and he should go for remedial mini courses to strengthen his entering level of competence. When he believes that he is ready to take the entry test again, he may be allowed to take the test and may be further allowed to proceed to the pre-test, if found competent enough. Then comes the pre-test, which is again an objective type test. It helps to self-evaluate the student's status when he proceeds with the module. It is followed by introduction of the topic. General and specific objectives are delineated in behavioural terms. Next, the learning materials for objectives I and II are presented. Necessary diagrams, sketches, pictures, work sheets, examples, dimensional drawings, practicum and project work etc., are included in the materials suitably.

Since module is a self instructional package, there is a greater need for formative evaluation, to measure the progress and guide the content and pace of the lessons. Formative evaluation is done to discover the strengths and weaknesses in learning to make midcourse corrections, in pace or content of instruction (Slavin, 1987). In the modules, provision is made for formative evaluation in the form of embedded tests. These tests are useful to the degree that it is informative, closely tied to the curriculum being taught, timely and frequent. Also, they provide feed back' to the students that they can use to improve their learning. After all the learning materials are presented, a post-test is given. This is also of objective type in nature. It is used to make summative evaluation of students' knowledge or skills. It allows for comparison among students. Necessary bibliographical references, assignments and guidelines for further follow up action are also furnished in the modules. Practicum and project works listed out in the modules promote learning by doing, field trips, experimentation and above all, the involvement of the students which, interacting with one another, ameliorate smooth learning, deepen understanding, lengthen retention and facilitate transfer or recall. Finally, keys to all the tests are appended at the end.

The above provisions enable the students to make self study with the help of the modules. The modules thus, developed were keenly edited with reference to accuracy and relevance of the material, style, vocabulary, density of presenting the facts and content interest. This scanning was very useful to eliminate ambiguities, obscurities and other inadequacies. It also helped to improve the logical sequence of the presentation and also to improve the technical accuracy of the content presented. For proper editing of the modules, the services of the colleagues and subject experts in the respective disciplines were utilised.

Once the editing was over, the modules were ready for try-outs. Try-out is an essential process of validation and the try-outs help in refining the module and make it relevant to the target population. So the modules prepared for this study were subjected to individual as well as group try-outs.

In the individual try-out, the researcher sat face to face with the randomly selected individuals of the target students one at a time. This gave him an opportunity to study the reactions of the learner in respect to the materials presented. He noted down the time taken for reading and understanding. Clarification asked, remarks made and the pre-test and the post-test scores were also noted down. On the basis of these ratings and analysis of the tryout, necessary corrections, modifications, refinements etc., were made then and there itself. Thus after completion of ten individual tryouts, the material became better refined.

After this, the developed modules were subjected to a group tryout. The group contained students of the same target population. Separate answer sheets were provided for writing the answers to the pre-test and the post-test items. Sufficient time was given for the students to use the module and answer the questions. Congenial atmosphere was created and proper rapport was established since these are the requirements of any group tryout. The students were instructed about the nature of this auto instructional material and what is expected of them alongwith the purpose of this tryout. The reactions of the students during the tryout were noted down. Answer sheets of the students were finally evaluated for finding out the per centage of incorrect responses and their level of mastery achievement. On the basis these ratings and analysis of the tryout, required correction, modifications, refinements etc., were made wherever necessary. Both the tryouts ensured better refinement and perfection of modules. The agreement of views of experts who reviewed the modules was taken as the index of validity of the content of the modules. One specimen module for each subject is given in Appendix-I.

DEVELOPMENT OF MULTIMEDIA PACKAGES

After developing the modules, the investigator had to shoulder the Herculean task of providing multimedia base to the prepared modules. Every possible effort was taken to develop LTIM for each module prepared by the investigator. It ranged from colour chart to Thermocol Model. The list of LTIM and HTIM used in this study are given in Appendix-II. Video cassettes had been procured from the International Educational Research Centre, New Delhi for this purpose before hand. Similarly, audio cassettes had also been procured from commercial agencies for this purpose. For maths one cassette on "Equations" and another on "Cube", for science/two cassettes on "Chromosomes", one cassette on "Photosynthesis", two cassettes on "Science Experiments" were purchased, ACE audio cassettes were purchased covering the entire science units. Even then all the units could not be covered. Some of the cassettes were of high standard suitable to high school and higher secondary students only. So, there was need to develop video and audio cassettes by the researcher himself to provide multimedia base to the developed modules.

Video Recording and Shooting

Though the audio and video cassettes were played to the slow learners as and when required, to maintain logical sequence, they were recorded in proper sequential order. For the units not covered by the readymade audio-video cassettes, the investigator had to resort to video shooting and editing. Outstanding teachers of meritorious service were selected for this purpose to present the modular lesson as per the instructional direction of the investigator. All the selected subject resource persons hold master degrees in their respective subjects and in teaching. A professional videographer was employed for shooting. The shooting was done in the classroom of the school where the experiment was actually carried out. Though, we could not ensure a foolproof studio environment, every possible effort was taken to make the instructional presentation as lively as possible.

For science, bio-visual colour charts, and other LTIM and HTIM equipments were used. The key words were written on the black board to accentuate the visual impact. As the teacher presented his instructional content, the students could see the key words on the black board beside or beneath the chart or diagram. In this method, they could play back the tape as many times as they needed and see the key words and listen to the verbal exposition of the teacher. Simple experiments were done in the course of the instructional presentation which were also recorded in close up shots. The chemistry and physics experiments have been recorded in such a manner that the students can perform the same experiments, just by watching the experiments on the T.V. screen with the required apparatus and tools.

For mathematics, a step by step explanation was given by the teacher and wherever he gave assignments, the videographer printed a word display *i.e.,* use still/pause. So the students using this video lesson could make use of still/pause provision as and when the assignments appeared on the T.V. screen and they could complete the assignments at their own pace. For social science, all the key words were written on the black board below the chart and the teacher followed a logical presentation of instructional materials covering a sub-head at a time. The teacher and the relevant key words were at the focus always. For defence organisation in India, a unit covered under social science, live telecast of Republic day celebration was made use of to record the portions pertaining to Army, Air Force, Territorial Army, Border Security Force, Home Guards and the three wings of National Cadet Corps, the vital sub-heads in the selected unit. For navy, mixing was done by using vital pictures.

For English, all the key concepts were written on the black board and the teacher gave verbal explanation of each concept. As he was explaining, the video shooting was done bringing the teacher and concept being taught into the focus. Whenever there was power failure, which was of course, frequent, we used a generator for power supply which we had hired before hand for this purpose. It took four days to accomplish the task. The shots were made according to the description of scenes such as Long Shot (L.S.) Medium Shot (M.S.) Close-up Shot (C.S.), Zoom In (Z.I.) and Zoom Out (Z.O.).

4.2.2. Editing

Editing was done in the studio with the help of the videographer. The investigator and the subject experts were duly consulted in the editing process. It took a week for editing. The duration of each final cassette was two hours each. The approximate cost for developing the video programme was about four thousand rupees. The video programme covers nearly all the modules developed for the specified units. After a thorough and meticulous editing, the video cassettes were made ready for instructional presentation to the slow learners of class VIII.

Audio Recording

Having completed the video programme, the investigator had to develop audio cassettes for the specified units. The audio lecture was based on the developed modules. Since audio recording was comparatively less expensive the teachers were instructed to be more elaborative in their presentation. At the same time, they were advised also to set the pace of presentation so as to suit the slow learners. The duration of each of the five final cassettes was an hour.

Development of Computer Software for CAI

Since a multimedia approach would be incomplete without application of computer software, an earnest effort was made to develop computer software for CAI. A computer expert was consulted for this purpose and it was discussed with him how to develop software for CAI based on the modules. Though, there are various CAI programmes such as "drill and practice programme", "tutorial programmes", the investigator decided to follow the first one *i.e.*, drill and practice programme since this is the most widely used type of computer programme (Slavin 1986). The purpose of this programme was to provide practice on skills and knowledge so that students can remember and use what they have been taught. The methodology involves repetition of a format in which the computer presents an exercise, the student types in a response, and the computer informs the student if the answer is correct. Diagrams and sketches were also incorporated in the software in appropriate places through scanning procedure. For subjects and units different codes were allotted. The software was prepared in such a way that it ensured the following:

(1) Letting students work at their own pace.

(2) Providing immediate feed back and reinforcement.

(3) Measuring performance quickly and giving students information on their performance.

The cost of the software was Rs. 3000 since they charge at exorbitant rate for development of software in Tamil Language, which is a rare phenomenon here. The software had to be developed in Tamil language since it was meant for Tamil medium students. Once the programming was over, it was subjected to tryouts. In the tryouts the students expressed that it was more conducive for learning at their own pace. Also, they found it more effective since the interaction with the computer had a motivating quality of its own. After this, the software for CAI programme was made ready for the use of the experimental group slow learners.

Multimedia Modular Plan

At the start, an entry test is given to students to determine their own entering levels of competence. If a student fails to obtain the prescribed minimum level of competence or achievement, he should go for remedial mini courses to strengthen his level of competence. Others can proceed with the module. Those who do not make it, should get their entering levels of competence strengthened by way of remedial mini course and then they can proceed to the pre-test. Pre-test helps to self evaluate the student's status when he proceeds with the module. Then they peruse the learning materials for general objectives. Their learning is accentuated by media as well as teacher support. Next their learning is assessed by means of a formative evaluation in the form of embedded test. After this, the students study the learning materials presented for specific objectives. They are adequately provided with media and teacher support to facilitate better learning. Then a formative evaluation of specific objectives is done. It is followed by practicum and project activities related to the concept dealt with. These provide for experimentation and work experience which, in turn, facilitate learning by doing. Lastly, a summative evaluation is done in the form of a post-test or modular test. Those who fail to obtain the specified mastery level in the post-test should again go for remedial courses and they can take the test again when they feel confident and competent. Thus in the modular plan every student will be able to attain the specified mastery level, though the time taken may vary from student to student. The modular plan is presented in the form of a flow chart in the succeeding page.

Flow Chart of a Multimedia Modular Plan Based on This Study
A Ten Stage Plan

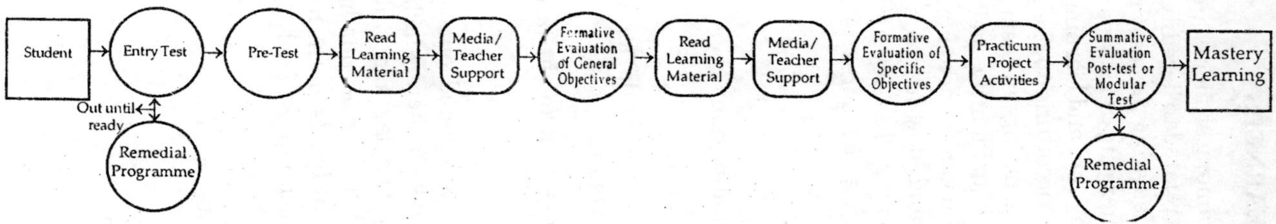

IDENTIFYING SLOW LEARNERS

Individual differences among students are found on account of certain operating factors related to heredity and environment. But, when we analyse the learning process of students, we find individual differences emerging on three grounds namely entering behaviour, learning rate and learning style. If a teacher sets his pace of instruction according to the needs of his more able students, those with learning problems can never catch up. So there is a greater need to identify students with learning problems so that instruction can be accommodated to student differences. Fast learners and slow learners can be identified on the basis of rate of learning. Tansley and Gulliford (1962) have laid down the following measures to identify the slow learners:

(1) Medical Examination

(2) A Psychological Examination:

  (a) Terman-Merrill Scale,

  (b) Wechsler Intelligence Scale for Children (WISC) (11 years to 16 years).

(3) An educational assessment (eight factors).

(4) A social history of the child.

Chintamani Kar (1992) has listed out certain tools and techniques to identify the slow learners which also conform to the measures laid down by Tansley and Gulliford. The only difference is what they classified under one head Chintamani Kar has placed under different heads on the basis of analytical classification. The tools and techniques listed out by Chintamani Kar are as follows:

(1) Observation technique

(2) Case study method

(3) Medical examination

(4) Scholastic tests

(5) Personality test

(6) Intelligence test

(7) Psychometric and psychological test

As far as this study is concerned, the investigator has followed a three phase process to identify the slow learners. They are:

(1) Identifying phase

(2) Scientific confirmatory phase

(3) Counter check phase.

Identifying Phase

For the first phase, the third measure recommended by Tansley and Gulliford (1962) which incorporates the first, second and fourth measures of Chintamani Kar has been followed:

An educational assessment of the students bring to light the slow learners. This educational assessment was made with the help of the concerned class teachers who spend most of the time with those students, by direct observation and by scrutiny of relevant school records. This type of educational assessment provides a detailed description of the child in the school setting, giving information about the eight factors:

(1) The child's level of attainment in the basic subjects in terms of what he can do and what his special difficulties appear to be.

(2) The child's level of language development and speech.

(3) Standards of achievement in other areas of curriculum *e.g.*, art, practical subject, physical education.

(4) Emotional and social behaviour as displayed both in and out of the classroom.

(5) Interest in and attitude towards school.

(6) Previous school history.

(7) The child's interest and background knowledge.

(8) Degree of parental co-operation.

By making an educational assessment of the target population by observation technique as well as by scrutiny of records, which gave a subtle insight into the students capacity and achievement, about 60 slow learners were identified in the first phase.

Scientific Confirmatory Phase

The slow learners identified in the aforesaid manner were, then, subjected to a scientific confirmatory test. For this purpose Standard Progressive Matrices designed by Raven and successfully and effectively used by Soundararaja Rao and Rajaguru (1995) in Indian setting to identify slow learners in their study, was administered to the students as a scientific confirmatory test, even though there are other tests like Terman-Merrill Scale and Wechsler Intelligence Scale for Children (WISC -11 years to 16 years)

The Standard Progressive Matrices, sets A, B, C, D and E designed by J.C. Raven is a test of a person's capacity at the time of the test to apprehend meaningless figures presented for his observation, see the relationship between them, conceive the nature of the figures completing each system of relations presented, and by so doing, develop a systematic method of reasoning.

The scale consists of 60 problems divided into five sets of 12. In each set the first problem is as nearly as possible self evident. The problems which follow become progressively more difficult. The order of the tests provides the standard training in the method of working. The five sets provide five opportunities for grasping the method and five progressive assessments of a person's capacity for intellectual activity. Everyone is given exactly the same series of the problems in the same order and is asked to work at his own speed, without interruption, from the beginning to the end of the scale. A person's total score provides an index of his intellectual capacity.

Standard Progressive Matrices test was administered to the identified slow learners. The students were explained how to grasp each problem and how to find the right bit to complete the pattern. Apart from this, no assistance was given to the students in the method of working, as the standard order in which the problems are presented provides the necessary training.

The score obtained by each student and the time taken by each student to complete the test were noted down. In the confirmatory test, those who got less score (9-15/60 or below 25th per centile point) and took more time were classified as slow learners. In the confirmatory test, some of them turned out to be under achievers. Such students were excluded from the list of slow learners.

Countercheck Phase

The last phase was countercheck phase. Kirk (1962) took "rate of learning" as the basis for identifying slow learners. According to him, the slow learners, gifted and average children can be classified on the basis of their "rate of learning". He also strictly refused to equate the slow learners with mentally retarded because the former is capable of achieving a moderate degree of academic success eventhough at a slower rate than the average child. To determine their rate of learning a memory poem in their syllabus with 12 lines which had not been taught so far, was taught in detail and the students were instructed to write the poem without mistakes and the time taken by each student was noted down. The bright students took less time, the average students took about half an hour while the slow learners couldn't make it even in an hour time.

This procedure was repeated with a passage from science subject as well as social science subject. This gave them an opportunity to learn two specified passages in their mother tongue. Here, the proposition of Bloom was followed. In 1968 Bloom proposed that rather than providing all students with same amount of instructional time and allowing learning to differ, perhaps we should require that all or almost all students reach certain level of achievement by allowing time to differ.

That is, Bloom suggests that we give students as much time and instruction as necessary to bring them all to a reasonable level of learning.

Accordingly 80 per cent mastery level was fixed as expected mastery level. A specific passage from science as well as from social science subject was taught by the teacher. Then the students were instructed to make a thorough study of the passages. To ascertain their mastery, 25 objective type test items were framed based on the passages dealt with. Then the time taken by each student to get 80 per cent score was noted down by the investigator. The time taken by each student to attain 80 per cent mastery level signified his rate of learning. Naturally slow learners took three to four times more time to attain the specified mastery level than average and bright students. It was counterchecked whether it tallied with the list already prepared and it was found to do so. Ultimately 50 slow learners, who had taken more time were finalised as the slow learners required for the study to constitute the control group and the experimental group. In this context it can be stated that Sandras Checklist can also be used to countercheck the slow learners.

CONSTRUCTION OF TOOLS

To evaluate the effectiveness of multimedia based modules and to compare the achievement of the slow learners taught through multimedia based modular approach with that of control group as well as normal group, an achievement test was constructed. The test was constructed covering all the four subjects chosen for this study. Equal weightage was given to each subject. For each subject only three units were selected for the purpose of this study.

Questions of objective type nature were framed without omitting any unit. Multiple choice, fill in the blanks and match the following were the types of questions used in this achievement test. The questions were framed so as to suit the level of VIIIth standard students. Utmost care was taken to avoid ambiguity and ambivalences. The items included in the final form of achievement test were selected on the basis of item analysis.

Initially 120 questions of objective type in nature were framed for tryouts. Forty per cent multiple choice question items, forty per cent fill in the blanks or supply test items and twenty per cent matching test items were framed for the achievement test. Multiple choice test items were composed of a stem followed by a series of possible responses or options. The stem is a direct question or an incomplete statement with four options of which only one is the correct response. Due importance and weightage the investigator has given to multiple choice-test item because its level of difficulty can be varied with relative ease, and it is capable of reflecting simple student behavioural patterns such as recall of information as well as complex student behavioural patterns such as the ability to analyse and synthesise.

Supply test items or fill in the blank test items constitute 40 per cent of the achievement test items. These test items are questions or incomplete statements which require highly short and specific answers. The answer is usually a significant word or expression. Matching test items consist of two list of items and a set of instructions for matching one of the items in the first list with one of the items in the second list.

Item Analysis

After this pool of 120 test items was constructed, the framed test items were subjected to careful scrutiny and critical judgement by a panel of subject experts. Each item was critically examined for what might be termed "formal defects". The next stage was tryout, the whole pool of items was given as a test to 20 students belonging to the target population. The obtained data were then used for an elaborate set of statistical procedures known as item analysis which gave the investigator informations regarding:

(1) Item difficulty

(2) Item discrimination

(3) Error or distraction analysis.

Test Item Difficulty

Test item difficulty refers to the per centage of students who correctly answer to a given test item. The level of difficulty was determined by using the formula

$$P = \frac{N_r}{N_t} \times 100$$

where,

P = Per centage of students who answered the test item correctly

N_r = Number of students who answered the test item correctly

N_t = Total number of students who attempted to answer the test item

In most of the cases the per centage clustered around the 50 per cent level. On the basis of this analysis, too easy and too difficult test items were deleted in the final form of achievement test.

Test Item Discriminating Power

A test item possesses adequate discriminating power when it is capable of differentiating between superior and inferior students. To determine item discriminating power the following simple formula was used even though there are many different computational schemes

$$D = \frac{U - L}{N}$$

where

D = Index of item discriminating power

U = Number of students in the upper group who answer the test item correctly (usually 27% of the total group)

L = Number of students in the lower group who answer the test items correctly (usually 27% of the total group)

N = Number of students in each group.

For more than 50 per cent of the test items, the computed D value exceeded +0.4 which indicated that the test items were good and for the remaining items, the computed 'D' value ranged between +0.40 and +0.20 which was a clear indication to the satisfactory condition of the test item. Those items which failed to differentiate between the superior and the inferior students were not included in the final form of achievement test. The P-value and D-value for each of the 120 test items in the initial form of achievement test were calculated and they are given in Appendix-III. The final form of achievement test is given in Appendix-IV.

Each item was scored 'one' mark for the correct response and 'zero' mark for the wrong response. The duration of the test was 2 hours. The same achievement test was used as pre-test and post-test and retention test in the study for all the three groups mentioned in the study. The English version of the final form of achievement test is given in Appendix-V.

Pre-Testing

Then a pre-testing was made administering the test to twenty students belonging to the target population. The main purpose of the pre-testing was to establish the reliability of the achievement test. The scores obtained by the students in the pre-testing formed the basis for establishing reliability of the test.

RELIABILITY OF THE TOOL USED

The test reliability means the consistency with which a set of test scores measures what they do measure (Ebel. 1975). It relates to the accuracy with which skills and knowledge are measured (Slavin, 1987). Reliability is a necessary condition for validity. Reliability co-efficient provides the most revealing statistical index of validity that is ordinarily available.

There are different methods to estimate the reliability of a test. Some of the commonly used methods are:

(1) Test-retest reliability,

(2) Split half reliability,

(3) Alternative parallel form reliability, and

(4) Kuder-Richardson Estimates.

In the present study, the split half method is used to estimate the reliability of the test. The split half method is considered to be one of the best methods for measuring reliability because all the data for computing reliability are obtained by one testing. Also, the variations likely to be brought about by difference between the two testing situations are eliminated.

The test was conducted to twenty VIII th standard students. In this method, the test items were divided into two equivalent halves by pooling the scores on odd numbered items and then pooling the scores on even numbered items, and the correction was found for these half tests by using the Karl Pearson's correlation coefficient formula,

$$r = \frac{N\Sigma \times Y - \Sigma \times \Sigma Y}{\sqrt{[N\Sigma X^2 - (\Sigma X)^2][N\Sigma Y^2 - (\Sigma Y)^2]}}$$

$$= \frac{20 \times 9894 - 431 \times 434}{\sqrt{[20 \times 9987 - 185761]}\ \sqrt{[20 \times 10096 - 188356]}}$$

$$= \frac{197880 - 187054}{\sqrt{[199740 - 185761]}\ \sqrt{[201920 - 188356]}}$$

$$= \frac{10826}{\sqrt{13979}\ \sqrt{13564}}$$

$$= \frac{10826}{13769}$$

r = 0.78 (The obtained r value is high and positive)

From the reliability of half test correlation, the self-correlation of the whole test is then estimated by using Spearman-Brown's Prophecy Formula.

$$r_{xx} = \frac{2\,r_{oe}}{1 + r_{oe}}$$

$$= \frac{2 \times 0.78}{1 + 0.78}$$

$$= \frac{1.56}{1.78}$$

$r_{xx} = 0.88$

Where r_{xx} = coefficient of Internal consistency

r_{oe} = coefficient of correlation between the odd-half scores and even-half scores

(The obtained r_{xx} value indicates that coefficient of internal consistency is high and positive.)

VALIDITY OF THE TOOLS USED

A research tool is said to be valid when it measures what it purports to measure. Any achievement test should possess validity. Validity indicates how adequately the content of the test is sampling that domain about which inferences are to be made. It is particularly very important for achievement test. A logical examination of instructional objectives and the contents to be taught was done by a panel of experts. The panel consisted of one professor in Education, one lecturer from physics department of our Alagappa University, one professor from ANJA College, Sivakasi and four noteworthy P.G. Assistants of Rajapalayam taluk in addition to the P.G. Teachers serving in the school where the experiment was carried out. The agreement of the views of the ten experts was taken as the index of validity of the content of achievement test.

The developed modules and the multimedia packages were also viewed by the same panel of experts. The experts who perused the modules expressed their view that the modules would be easier than the text book. Also, they viewed the multimedia packages like audio and video cassettes and CAI software and were of unanimous opinion that the multimedia packages were relevant to the instructional content and they had the anticipated aural and visual effect besides having a motivating quality of their own. The agreement of the views of the panel experts was taken as the index of validity of the modules and multimedia packages. The achievement test constructed by the investigator was subjected to scrutiny by experts. The agreement of views of those experts made the base for content validity and reliability of the test was estimated using split half method and then by applying Karl Pearson's Correlation Co-efficient formula.

SAMPLE OF THE STUDY

For the purpose of investigation, 50 slow learners of VIII standard from S.S.H.N. Higher Secondary School, Muhavur were selected. The slow learners were identified by educational assessment and then they were subjected to a confirmatory test. Standard Progressive Matrices test was administered to them to scientifically confirm the identification. In the third phase, they were counter-checked on the basis of "learning rate". Finally selected slow learners were divided into two halves to constitute the control group and the experimental group.

Description of the Sample and Sampling Technique

Out of the fifty students finally selected for the study two groups were formed following systematic random sampling technique. They were placed in the order of merit based on their performance in Standard Progressive Matrices Test. All the odd number students formed the control group while the even number students constituted the experimental group. The control group was taught through traditional lecture method while the experimental group was taught through multimedia based modular approach.

Procedure for Equating the Groups

The sample of 50 students was divided into two equated groups of 25 students each. The two groups were equated as nearly as possible in terms of their achievement scores in the Standard Progressive Matrices Test. Students having similar range of marks in the confirmatory test were allotted equally and randomly for experimental and control groups. To find out whether the control group and the experimental group are matched ones or not mean and standard deviation were calculated for the scores obtained in RPM test by each group. Then t-test was applied to the scores of control group and experimental group. The obtained t- value was found to be not significant (t-value 0.82) at 0.05 level and hence, the two groups were matched ones in terms of their achievement before the inception of the experimental study.

Also t-test was applied to the pre-test scores to verify, whether these groups were matched ones. The obtained t-value (t-value 0.57) was not significant at 0.01 level. Thus, both the t-tests revealed that the two groups were matched ones before the inception of experimentation.

TEACHING BY MULTIMEDIA BASED MODULAR APPROACH

The experimental group slow learners were taught through multimedia based modular approach for a period of 45 working days at the rate of one and half hours per day especially in the evening after the class hours. The students were taught by Low Technology Instructional Media (LTIM) and High Technology Instructional Media (HTIM). Audio and video cassettes were played to the slow learners as and when required. The CAI software was also used on turn basis since we could not provide sufficient number of computers. Twelve units were covered inclusive of the four specified subjects during the period of investigation. For 12 units, 40 modules had been developed.

The control group as well as the normal group students were taught through the traditional lecture method by the regular teachers in the normal class hours. The experimental group slow learners were encouraged to make self study with the help of the multimedia based modules. They were also advised to use the modules strictly as per the instructions given in the modules. All the modules were arranged in sequential order and they were supplied to the experimental group slow learners in the form of a handbook. The slow learners of the experimental group were not allowed to take the handbook (Modules) home, since there was every possibility for the students of normal group and the slow learners of the control group to go through the modules or to get them xeroxed, which would ultimately distort the result of the study.

For conducting the experiments the biology lab was chosen. Everyday the audio and the video cassettes were played to the students of experimental group covering the module they studied on that particular day. CAI software was also used for the benefits of the slow learners of the experimental group. Though the students had some problems initially with the code number and with the key board, since they did not know how to handle the key board, they picked up the modus operandi in a week or so.

Since CAI software had a motivating quality of its own, due to the provisions for interaction by students, the slow learners were very much attracted to it. The provision for knowledge of result, immediate feed back and reinforcement found in the CAI programme made their learning exciting and pleasant. As in the printed text, there was no need for the slow learners to scan the text to find out the correct response, which was furnished by the computer itself in the CAI programme. The diagrams and the sketches which were incorporated in the CAI software through scanning procedure, made good visual impact which, in turn, contributed for better understanding and longer retention.

Besides using audio, video and CAI software the slow learners were encouraged to do simple experiments specified in the practicum and project work. Everyday all possible equipments and apparatus were provided to the experimental group slow learners to try their hands in doing simple experiments. Watching the experiments done by the teacher on the TV screen, they were able to do the same by themselves. This video programme was found to have imbibed a sense of self-confidence in them. When enough apparatus and tools were not available for all the slow learners, they were advised to do the experiments as a group. For complex experiments also, the same procedure was adapted.

The teacher support system was restricted to the extent of aiding the students in the operation of HTIM equipments, clarifying doubts of the experimental group slow learners and guiding the students in experiments and the project works. After a period of forty five working days, a post-test was conducted for all the three groups. After a lapse of two months from the date of post-test, a retention test was administered to all the three groups.

DATA COLLECTION

At the end of the experimental period, a post-test was conducted to the slow learners of the experimental group and the control group and the students of the normal group. Exactly two months after that again a retention test was administered to all the three 'groups to measure their degree of retention. The responses given by the students in the pre-test, post-test and the retention test formed the vital data required for the analysis. The scores of the three groups in the pre-test, post-test and retention test are given in Appendix-VIII. In addition to that, subjectwise scores of all the three groups are furnished in appendices from IX to XI.

SCORING PROCEDURE

The achievement test consisted of 100 objective type questions, the total score of the test is 100. For each correct answer, the score is one and for each wrong answer the score is zero. The answer key to the achievement test is given in Appendix-VI. English version of the key to the achievement test is given in Appendix-VII.

STATISTICAL TECHNIQUES USED IN THE STUDY

The data thus obtained were analysed by using appropriate statistical techniques such as mean standard deviation and t-test. The details of analysis and interpretation are presented in the succeeding chapter.

5

RESULTS AND DISCUSSION

The application of statistical techniques in analysing and interpreting the collected data plays an important role in any research problem. The data must be carefully processed, systematically classified and tabulated, scientifically analysed and rationally concluded. This chapter deals with the analysis of data collected for the study. The effectiveness of multimedia based modular approach was measured through an achievement test with a set of 100 objective type test items. Each item in the achievement test carries 'one' mark for right response and 'zero' for wrong response. The same achievement test as well as the same scoring procedure was used to measure the effectiveness of the Traditional Lecture Method also.

Before giving treatment to the slow learners of the experimental group, a pre-test was conducted to the students of all the three groups. The total score obtained by each respondent in the achievement test was calculated. After implementing Multimedia Based Modular Approach for a period of 45 working days, a post-test was conducted to all the groups. Then, after a lapse of two months period, the same achievement test was once again administered to the students of all the three groups in order to assess whether the multimedia based modular approach is able to sustain or promote retention in the minds of the students

Based on the total score of each subject and subjects as a whole, mean and standard deviation for pre-test, post-test and retention test for each group *i.e.,* normal group, control group and experimental group were calculated. Based on the mean and standard deviation, t-test was applied to know the significant difference, if any, in the achievement of control group slow learners, experimental group slow learners and the normal group students.

The analysis of data and the findings are presented in the form of tables.

Comparison of Pre-test Mean Scores of Control Group Slow Learners and Experimental Group Slow Learners

Mean and standard deviation of the pre-test scores of the control group and experimental group slow learners and the calculated t-value are presented in Table-1.

Table-1: Mean and Standard Deviation of Pre-test Scores of Control Group Slow Learners and Experimental Group Slow Learners and the Calculated t-value.

Name of the Group	N	Mean	S.D.	Calculated t-value
Control Group	25	19.8	4.8	0.57 @
Experimental Group	25	20.6	5.25	

Note: @ Not significant at 0.05 level.

From Table-1, it is seen that the obtained t-value (0.57) is not significant at 0.05 level. It indicates that there is no variation in the achievement of control group and experimental group slow learners in the pre-test performance. Hence, the formulated hypothesis that there exists no significant difference between the pre-test mean scores of control group slow learners and experimental group slow learners is accepted.

From the above, it is concluded that there is no significant difference between the pre-test means scores of control group and experimental group slow learners and both the control group and experimental group were matched ones before the experiment. Also, it testifies to reliability of the classification of the matched groups on the basis of half yearly examination scores and RPM scores.

Comparison of Pre-test Mean Scores of Control Group Slow Learners and Normal Group Students

Mean and standard deviation of pre-test scores of control group slow learners and normal group students and the calculated t-value are presented in Table-2.

Table-2: Mean and Standard Deviation of Pre-test Scores of Control Group Slow Learners and Normal Group Students and Calculated t-value.

Name of the Group	N	Mean	S.D.	Calculated t-value
Control Group	25	19.8	4.8	16.00 **
Normal Group	25	47.0	7.14	

Note: ** Significant at 0.01 level.

From Table-2, it is observed that the obtained t-value (16.00) is significant at 0.01 level. It evinces that there existed a gulf of difference between the achievements of control group slow learners and normal group students. Therefore, the formulated hypothesis that there exists significant difference between the pre-test mean scores of control group slow learners and normal group students is accepted.

From this analysis, it is concluded that there exists significant difference between the pre-test means scores of control group slow learners and the normal group students. Also, the achievement of normal group students is higher than the achievement of control group slow learners.

Comparison of Pre-test Mean Scores of Experimental Group Slow Learners and Normal Group Students

Mean and standard deviation of pre-test scores of experimental group slow learners and normal group students and the calculated t-value are presented in Table-3.

Table-3: Mean and Standard Deviation of Pre-test Scores of Experimental Group Slow Learners and Normal Group Students and the Calculated t-value.

Name of the Group	N	Mean	S.D.	Calculated t-value
Control Group	25	20.6	5.25	14.92 **
Normal Group	25	47.0	7.14	

Note: ** Significant at 0.01 level.

From Table-3, it is noticed that the obtained t-value (14.92) is significant at 0.01 level. It testifies to the fact that there existed a gulf of difference between the achievements of experimental group slow learners and the normal group students. Hence, the formulated hypothesis that there exists significant difference between the pre-test mean scores of experimental group slow learners and normal group students is accepted.

Further, the mean value (47) obtained by the normal group students in the pre-test reveals that their achievement in the pre-test was higher than the achievement of the experimental group slow learners (20.6). It implies that the normal group students showed tremendous achievement and superemacy over the experimental group slow learners.

From the above, it is concluded that there is significant difference between the achievements of experimental group slow learners and the normal group students in the pre-test. The achievement of normal group students is higher than the achievement of experimental group slow learners.

Comparison of Pre-test and Post-test Mean Scores of Control Group Slow Learners taught through Traditional Lecture Method

Mean and standard deviation of the pre-test and post-test scores of experimental group slow learners and the calculated t-value are presented in Table-4

Table-4: Mean and Standard Deviation of the Pre-test and Post-test Scores of Experimental Group Slow Learners and the Calculated t-value.

Name of the Test	N	Mean	S.D.	Calculated t-value
Pre-test	25	19.8	4.8	1.94@
Post-test	25	22.8	6.0	

Note: @ Not Significant at 0.05 level.

From Table-4, it is clear that the obtained t-value (1.94) is not significant at 0.05 level. It shows that the control group slow learners of Std. VIII could not improve significantly their understanding and mastery of the subject units, when they were taught through traditional lecture method. Hence, the formulated hypothesis that there exists no significant difference between the pre-test and post-test mean scores of control group slow learners when the subjects are taught through traditional lecture method is accepted.

However, the mean values obtained by the slow learners of the control group in the pre-test and post-test reveal that their achievement is higher in the post-test (Mean value: 22.8) than in the pre-test (Mean value 19.8). It means that though the control group slow learners improved their means score in the post-test, they could not make any significant difference in their performance.

From the above, it is concluded that the control group slow learners could not show significant difference between the pre-test and post-test mean scores when they were taught through traditional lecture method. Their performance in the post-test was no better than their performance in the pre-test. It suggests that the traditional lecture method is not effective for slow learners and they need some other instructional strategy to evince a better performance.

Comparison of Pre-test and Post-test Mean Scores of Experimental Group Slow Learners Taught Through Multimedia Based Modular Approach

Presented below in Table-5 are the mean, standard deviation of the pre-test and post-test scores of experimental group slow learners and the calculated t-value.

Table-5: Mean and Standard Deviation of the Pre-test and Post-test Scores of Experimental Group Slow Learners and the Calculated t-value.

Name of the Test	N	Mean	S.D.	Calculated t-value
Pre-test	25	20.6	5.25	12.61 **
Post-test	25	46.2	8.70	

Note: ** Significant at 0.01 level.

From Table-5, it is understood that the obtained t-value (12.61) is significant at 0.01 level. It signifies that the experimental group slow learners significantly improved their learning and achievement after treatment through multimedia based modular approach. Hence, the formulated hypothesis that there exists significant difference between the pre-test and post-test mean scores of the slow learners in the experimental group when the subjects are taught through multimedia based modular approach is accepted.

Further, the mean values obtained by experimental group slow learners in the pre-test and post-test scores disclose that their achievement is higher in the post-test (mean value: 46.2) than in the pre-test (mean value: 20.6). It means that the experimental group slow learners have made a vertical progress in their performance in the post-test. Moreover, an analysis of rate of progress made by both control group and experimental group throws light on the effectiveness of modular approach with special reference to slow learners. From a meagre mean score of 20.6 in the pre-test, they could gain an impressive mean score of 46.2 in the post-test which is more than double the pre-test mean score. But, the control group slow learners could not make significant mean gain in the post-test. This vouchsafes the advantage of multimedia based modular approach over the traditional lecture method with special reference to slow learners.

From the above, it is concluded that the multimedia based modular approach significantly boosted up the performance of the experimental group slow learners. The achievement of experimental group slow learners is higher in the post-test than in the pre-test. It conforms to the findings of Gabriel, Pillai and Gnanam (1989), Ramar (1994), Postlethwat, Novah and Murray (1964), Rajaguru (1994) and Schmidt (1991) who all have established that multimedia based modular approach significantly enhanced the achievement of backward students such as low achievers and slow learners after the experimental treatment.

Comparison of Pre-test and Post-test Mean Scores of Normal Group Students Taught Through Traditional Lecture Method

Table-6 depicts the mean and standard deviation of the pre-test and post-test scores of normal group students and the calculated t-value.

Table-6: Mean and Standard Deviation of Pre-test and Post-test Scores of Normal Group Students and the Calculated t-value.

Name of the Test	N	Mean	S.D.	Calculated t-value
Pre-test	25	47.0	7.14	
				1.96
Post-test	25	51.2	8.00	

Note: @ Not Significant at 0.05 level.

From Table-6, it is understood that the obtained t-value (1.96) is not significant at 0.05 level. It points out that the normal group students did not improve their performance significantly when taught through traditional lecture method. So, the formulated hypothesis that there exists no significant difference between the pre-test and post-test mean scores of normal group students taught through traditional lecture method is accepted. Just as the traditional lecture method could not enable the control group slow learners to improve their learning significantly (ref. Table-4), it has done so with regard to normal group students also. This can be understood from the mean gains made by both the groups. While the control group made a mean gain of 3.0 for 19.8 (ref. Table-4), normal group obtained a mean gain of 4.2 for 47. The traditional lecture method could not lead them to better attainment in the post-test. From the above, it is concluded that there is no significant difference between the pre-test and post-test achievements of normal group students when taught through traditional lecture method.

Comparison of Post-test Mean Scores of Control Group Slow Learners Taught Through Traditional Lecture Method and Experimental Group Slow Learners Taught Through Multimedia Based Modular Approach

Table-6 shows the mean and standard deviation of the post-test scores of the control group slow learners and the experimental group slow learners and the calculated t-value.

Table-7: Mean and Standard Deviation of Post-test Scores of the Control Group and Experimental Group Slow Learners and the Calculated t-value.

Name of the Group	N	Mean	S.D.	Calculated t-value
Control Group	25	22.8	6.0	11.07**
Experimental Group	25	46.2	8.7	

Note: ** Significant at 0.01 level.

From Table-7, it is evident that the obt ined t-value (11.07) is significant at 0.01 level. It implies that the experimental group slow learners taught through multimedia based modular approach have shown significantly better performance than the control group slow learners taught through traditional Lecture method. Therefore, the formulated hypothesis that there exists significant difference between the post-test mean scores of the slow learners in the control group and the slow learners in the experimental group is accepted.

Further, the mean values obtained by the control group (22.8) and the experimental group (46.2) bring to light the progress made by them in learning. The rate of progress made by the experimental group slow learners is higher than the rate of progress made by the control group slow learners. In terms of per centage, the rate of progress shown by the experimental group slow learners taught through multimedia based modular approach is 124% (from 20.6 to 46.2) (ret. Table-5), while the rate of progress made by the control group slow learners is 15 % (from 19.9 to 22.8) (ref. Table-4). The difference in the rate of progress can be attributed to the operation of the experimental factor *i.e.*, implementation of multimedia based modular approach.

From the above, it is concluded that there is significant difference between the post-test performances of control group slow learners taught through traditional lecture method and the experimental group slow learners taught through multimedia based modular approach. The achievement of experimental group slow learners is higher than the achievement of control group slow learners. Moreover, the rate of progress made by the experimental group slow learner is higher than that of the control group slow learners. The variation in the rates of progress made by both the groups is the resultant product of multimedia based modular approach and it vouches for the effectiveness of multimedia based modular approach.

Comparison of Post-test Mean Scores of Slow Learning Boys and Slow Learning Girls in the Control Group Taught Through Traditional Lecture Method

Mean and standard deviation of the post-test scores of the control group boys and girls taught through traditional lecture method and the calculated t-value are presented in Table-8.

Table-8: Mean and Standard Deviation of Post-test Scores of the control Group Boys and Girls taught through Traditional Lecture Method and the Calculated t-value.

Category	N	Mean	S.D.	Calculated t-value
Boys	15	24.3	6.69	2.55*
Gins	10	20.5	3.35	

Note: * Significant at 0.05 level.

From Table-8, it is clear that the obtained t-value (2.55) is significant at 0.05 level. It indicates that there is significant difference between the achievements of the boys and girls in the control group taught through traditional lecture method. Hence, the formulated hypothesis that there exists significant difference between the post-test mean scores of the slow learning boys and the slow learning girls in the control group taught through traditional lecture method is accepted.

From the above, it is concluded that there is significant difference between the post-test performances of the slow learning boys and the slow learning girls in the control group taught through traditional lecture method. From the very meagre mean gain (from 18 to 20.5) made by the slow learning girls in the control group it is explicit that they could not make as much mean gain as the slow learning boys who made a mean gain of 4 from 20.3 to 24.3. This avers that the traditional lecture method is not effective to the slow learning girls and they need all the more a newer innovative method of instruction to show any significant difference in their performance.

Comparison of Post-test Mean Scores of Slow Learning Boys and Slow Learning Girls in the Experimental Group Taught Through Multimedia Based Modular Approach

Table-9 reflects mean and standard deviation of the post-test scores of the slow learning boys and slow learning girls in the experimental group taught through multimedia based modular approach and the calculated t-value.

Table-9: Mean and Standard Deviation of Post-test Scores of the Boys and Girls of the Experimental Group and the Calculated t-value.

Category in Post-test	N	Mean	S.D.	Calculated t-value
Boys	15	46.3	7.2	0.33@
Girls	10	45.5	9.8	

Note: @ Not Significant at 0.05 level.

From Table-9, it is observed that the obtained t-value (0.33) is not significant at 0.05 level. It indicates that there is no significant difference in the post-test performance of the boys and girls in the experimental group taught through multimedia based modular approach. Hence, the formulated hypothesis that there is significant difference between the post-test mean scores of the slow learning boys and slow learning girls in the experimental group is rejected.

From the above, it is concluded that, even though there was significant difference between the boys and girls of the control group in the post-test performance, there was no such significant difference between the slow learning boys and the slow learning girls in the experimental group in their post-test performance. While the girls in the matched control group trailed behind the boys, the girls in the experimental group were at par with boys in the post-test performance. This may be attributed to the effectiveness of multimedia based modular approach. This type of better performance of the girls will have far reaching effects like reducing the failures and dropouts of girl students and it will diminish to a great extent, wastage and stagnation in our schools.

Comparison of Post-test Mean Scores of Control Group Slow Learners and Normal Group Students

Table-10 shows the mean and standard deviation of the post-test scores of control group slow learners and the normal group students and the calculated t-value.

Table-10: Mean and Standard Deviation of Post-test Scores of the Control Group Slow Learners and the Normal Group Students and the Calculated t-value.

Name of the Group	N	Mean	S.D.	Calculated t-value
Control Group	25	22.8	6	14.2**
Normal Group	25	51.2	8	

Note: ** Significant at 0.01 level.

From Table-10, it is noticed that the obtained t-value (13.6) is significant at 01 level. It evinces that the normal group students performed significantly better than the control group slow learners. Hence, the formulated hypothesis that there exists significant difference between the post-test mean scores of the slow learners in the control group and the students in the normal group is accepted.

Further, the mean values (19.8 and 22.8) obtained by the control group slow learners reveal that, though they have made progress by traditional lecture method, they could not narrow down the gap between them and the normal students. The gulf of difference .between these two groups persisted in the post-test because the progress made by the control group slow learners in the post-test performance was insignificant. It means that the traditional lecture method could neither boost up the performance of control group slow learners nor enable them to cope with normal students.

From the above, it is concluded that there is significant difference between the post-test achievements of control group slow learners and the normal group students. The achievement of normal group students is higher than the achievement of control group slow learners. The traditional lecture method could not enable the control group slow learners to narrow down the gap that existed between them and the normal group students.

Comparison of Post-test Mean Scores of Experimental Group Slow Learners Taught Through Multimedia Based Modular Approach and the Normal Group Students

Mean and standard deviation of post-test scores of experimental group slow learners and the normal group students and the calculated t-value are presented in Table-11.

Table-11: Mean and Standard Deviation of Post-test Scores of Experimental Group Slow Learners and the Normal Group Students and the Calculated t-value.

Name of the Group	N	Mean	S.D.	Calculated t-value
Experimental Group	25	46.2	8.7	2.11*
Normal Group	25	51.0	8.0	

Note: * Significant at 0.05 level.

From Table-11, it is observed that the obtained t-value (2.11) is significant at 0.05 level. It implies that the normal group students showed significant variation in their performance and their achievement in the post-test is significantly higher than the achievement of experimental group slow learners. Hence, the formulated hypothesis that there exists no significant difference between the post-test mean scores of the slow learners in the experimental group and the students in the normal group is rejected.

However, a critical analysis of the mean values obtained by the experimental group slow learners in the post-test (46.2) and in the pre-test (20.6) throws light on the significant progress made by the experimental group slow learners after the experiment. The gulf of difference that existed between both the groups in the pre-test performance (Mean value of normal group 47.0) was narrowed down to a significant extent in the post-test performance, since both the groups obtained the mean values of 51.2 and 46.2 respectively.

Mean difference between the normal group students and the experimental group slow learners is 5 in Table-11. But the mean difference between the normal group students and the control group slow learners is 28.4 in Table-10. Rate of progress made by the experimental group slow learners is higher (124.7) than the rate of progress made by the normal group students (11.06%). These facts vouchsafe the advantage of multimedia based modular approach over the traditional lecture method.

The above analysis gives the conclusion that there is significant difference between the post-test performance scores of the experimental group slow learners and the normal group students. The achievement of the normal group students is higher than the achievement of experimental group slow learners. However, a critical analysis of the mean values signifies that the experimental group slow learners significantly improved their achievement after the experiment. Moreover, the multimedia based modular approach enabled the experimental group slow learners to cope with the normal students to a greater extent. The narrowed down gulf of difference between both the groups bears testimony to the effectiveness of multimedia based modular approach. Further, a comparative study of Table-10 and Table-11 testifies to the advantage of multimedia based modular approach over the traditional lecture method. It is in agreement with the findings of Schmidt (1991), Leitner (1992), Ramar (1994), Reddy and Ramar (1994,1995) and Postlethwat (1964) who have substantiated that CAI, video instruction and modular instructions could enable the backward students like low achievers and slow learners to cope with normal students taught through traditional lecture method.

Comparison of Post-test and Retention-test Scores of the Control Group Slow Learners

Mean and standard deviation of the post-test and retention test scores of control group and the calculated t-value are presented in Table-12.

Table-12: Mean and Standard Deviation of Post-test and Retention test Scores of Control Group and the Calculated t-value.

Name of the Test	N	Mean	S.D.	Calculated t-value
Post-test	25	22.8	6.0	0.23 @
Retention test	25	22.4	5.7	

Note: @ Not Significant at 0.05 level.

From Table-12, it is seen that the obtained t-value (0.23) is not significant at 0.05 level. It shows that there is no significant difference between the post-test performance and the retention test performance of control group slow learners. So, the formulated hypothesis that there is no significant difference between the post-test and retention test mean scores of the control group slow learners is accepted. The above analysis gives the conclusion that there is no significant difference in the achievements of control group slow learners between the post-test and retention test. It is observed that the mean value has decreased by 0.4. It indicates that the control group slow learners could not remember at the time of retention test all the facts and figures they were aware of at the post-test time. This ascribes for the decreased mean value in the retention test. The post-test score is higher than the retention test score in respect of most of the control group slow learners. The mean values of post-test and retention test further suggest that the traditional lecture method could neither contribute to nor promote retention.

Comparison of Post-test and Retention Test Scores of the Experimental Group Slow Learners

Mean and standard deviation of the post-test and retention test scores of control group and the calculated t-value are presented in Table-13.

Table-13: Mean and Standard Deviation of Post-test and Retention test Scores of Experimental Group and the Calculated t-value.

Name of the test	N	Mean	S.D.	Calculated t-value
Post-test	25	46.2	8.7	0.10@
Retention test	25	46.8	8.4	

Note: @ Not Significant at 0.05 level.

From Table-13, it is observed that the obtained t-value (0.10) is not significant at 0.05 level. It evinces that there is no significant difference between the post-test performance and the retention test performance of the experimental group slow learners. Hence, the formulated hypothesis that there exists no significant difference between the post-test and retention test mean scores of the slow learners in the experimental group is accepted.

However, a critical comparison of the retention test mean scores of experimental group with that of the pre-test brings to light certain interesting revelations. In case of control group slow learners the mean difference between pre-test and post-test is only 3 whereas the mean difference between pre-test and post-test in respect of experimental group slow learners is 25.6. Also, the experimental group slow learners could improve upon their post-test performance in the retention test. It indicates that they could retain more information than their counterparts.

From the above, it can be concluded that there is no significant difference between the post-test performance and retention test performance of experimental group slow learners. However, the significant mean difference (25.6) between the pre-test and post-test scores of experimental group slow learners highlights the volume of new additional informations acquired by them at the time of post-test. This fast learnt informations could be properly processed in their minds and kept in memory storage even after a period of two months without loss or distortion. This is well testified by the fact that the experimental group slow learners could improve upon their post-test performance in the retention test. Further, it substantiates that the multimedia based modular approach could contribute to and promote retention of slow learners. The better retention of experimental group slow learners is the resultant product of multimedia based modular treatment given to them during the period of experimentation. Also, it strengthens the findings of Hopper (1982) and Rajaguru (1994), Oberai (1981) and Kumar (1981) who have established that multimedia strategy and modular approach very much promote the retention of the students.

Comparison of Post-test and Retention Test Scores of the Normal Group Students

Table-14 depicts the mean, standard deviation of the post-test and retention test scores of normal group students and the calculated t-value.

Table-14: Mean and Standard Deviation of Post-test and Retention test Scores of Normal Group and the Calculated t-value.

Name of the test	N	Mean	S.D.	Calculated t-value
Post-test	25	50.0	8.0	0.18@
Retention test	25	49.2	6.68	

Note: @ Not Significant at 0.05 level.

From Table-14, it is understood that the obtained t-value (0.18) is not significant at 0.05 level. It shows that there is no significant difference in the achievements of normal group students between the post-test and retention test. So, the formulated hypothesis that there is no significant difference between the post-test and retention test mean scores of the normal group students is accepted.

The above analysis gives the conclusion that there is no significant difference between the post-test performance and the retention test performance of normal group students. It is noticed that the mean value has decreased by 0.0.8. It simply indicates that whatever informations they had in their minds at the time of post-test could not be recalled without loss or distortion at the time of retention test. This can be ascribed for their decreased mean value in the retention test. The post-test score is higher than the retention test score for most of the normal group students. A critical study of the mean values of the post-test and retention test further suggests that the traditional lecture method could neither promote retention nor facilitate transfer or recall.

Comparison of Retention Test Mean Scores of Slow Learning Boys and Slow Learning Girls in Control Group

Mean and standard deviation of the retention test scores of the slow learning boys and the slow learning girls in the control group and the calculated t-value are presented in Table-15.

Table-15: Mean and Standard Deviation of Retention Test Scores of Control Group Boys and Girls and the Calculated t-value.

Category	N	Mean	S.D.	Calculated t-value
Boys	15	25	6.78	2.27 *
Girls	10	21.5	3.9	

Note: * Significant at 0.05 level.

From Table-15, it is clear that the obtained t-value (2.27) is significant at 0.05 level. It indicates that the achievement of slow learning boys in the control group is higher than the achievement of slow learning girls. Hence, the formulated hypothesis that there is significant difference between the retention test mean scores of the slow learning boys and the slow learning girls in the control group is accepted. When the retention test t-value (2.27) of the control group boys and girls is compared with their post-test t-value (2.55), it is observed that the same degree of difference persists between the slow learning boys and slow learning girls. It also implies that both boys and girls of the control group could sustain the same degree of retention as they had in the post test till the retention test. Whatever facts and informations they had assimilated till the post-test, they could retain till the retention test. Also, even though the slow learning girls could narrow down the gap between them and the boys, the progress made by them is not significant. Hence, the significant difference between them persisted in the retention test also.

Comparison of Retention Test Mean Scores of the Slow Learning Boys and the Slow Learning Girls in the Experimental Group

Table-16 depicts the mean and standard deviation of retention test scores of the slow learning boys and the slow learning girls in the experimental group and the calculated t-value.

Table-16: Mean and Standard Deviation of Retention Test Scores of Experimental Group Boys and Girls and the Calculated t-value.

Category	N	Mean	S.D.	Calculated t-value
Boys	15	47	7.35	0.212@
Girls	10	46.5	9.23	

Note: @ Not Significant at 0.05 level.

From Table-16, it is evident that the obtained t-value (0.212) is not significant. It evinces that there is no significant difference in the retention test performance of the boys and the girls in the experimental group taught through multimedia based modular approach. Hence, the formulated hypothesis that there exists significant difference between the retention test mean scores of the slow learning boys and the slow learning girls in the experimental group is rejected.

From the above, it is concluded that both the slow learning boys and the slow learning girls in the experimental group are alike in retention power. Both the boys and girls in the experimental group have evinced same degree of retention by recalling the facts and concepts already learnt till the post-test at the time of retention test. The overcrowding of facts and the rapid acquisition of new informations and concepts during the period of experimentation did not affect their memory storage and retention. The very fact that the slow learners, who are known to be slow to "catch on", have been able to acquire this much of information in a short period and they have been able to retain them in memory for a considerable time testifies to the effectiveness of multimedia based modular approach.

The concrete presentation in the module which establishes the relevant association and relationship and repetition, revision, review and drill are certain factors which ameliorate the information processing in the minds of students. These factors helped the experimental group slow learners fix the concepts in their minds, without distortion and facilitated longer retention. That is why the slow learning boys and the slow learning girls in the experimental group could evince same degree of retention and so there was no significant difference in their retention test performance. It supports the findings of Madhur Gupta (1989), Oberai (1981), Kumar (1981) and Rajaguru (1994) who have established that multimedia instructional strategy promotes retention of the students.

Comparison of Pre-test and Post-test Mean Scores Analysis of all the Groups in English Subject

Table-17 reflects the mean and standard deviation of the pre-test and post-test scores of all the three groups and the calculated t-value.

Table-17: Mean and Standard Deviation of Pre-test and Post-test Scores of Control Group, Experimental Group and Normal Group and the Calculated t-values.

Name of Group	Pre-test			Post-test		Calculated
	N	M_1	$D.D_1$	M_2	$S.D_2$	t-value
Control Group	25	16.7	7.63	17.5	4.89	0.44@
Experimental Group	25	18.6	5.35	30.2	9.8	5.2 **
Normal Group	25	31.5	16.7	35.3	15.35	0.84@

Note: @ Not Significant at 0.05 level.

** Significant at 0.01 level.

From Tablo 17, it is observed that the t-values obtained in respect of control group and normal group (0.84 and 0.44) are not significant whereas the t- value (5.2) obtained in respect of experimental group is significant. It implies that the experimental group slow learners showed significant variation in their post-test and their achievement in the post-test is higher than their achievement in the pre-test. Hence, the formulated hypothesis that there exists significant difference between the pre-test and post-test mean scores of experimental group slow learners in English subject is accepted.

A critical analysis of mean values of all the three groups throws light on the effectiveness of multimedia based modular approach in teaching English to slow learners. In terms of per centage, the rate of progress made by the control group slow learners is 1.19%. Similarly, the rate of progress made by the experimental group slow learners is 64.4% which is tremendous and significant. This significant difference in the post-test achievement may be attributed to the effectiveness of multimedia based modular approach in teaching English to slow learners. The cumulative effect of the different components of multimedia accentuated the achievement of the slow learners in the experimental group. Moreover, the dual effect of audio and video strengthened their understanding of English usage, promoted longer retention and facilitated smooth recall. This information processing and retrieval ameliorated by the multimedia based modular approach, ultimately told upon the post-test performance of the experimental group slow learners.

From the above, it is concluded that there is significant difference between the pre-test and post-test mean scores of experimental group slow learners and their achievement is higher in the post-test than in the pre-test.

Moreover, the rate of progress made by the experimental group slow learners is more than the rate of progress made by the other two group students. It is in agreement with the findings of George (1966), Kumar (1981), Kasinathan (1992), Ramar (1994) and Natarajan (1996) who have highlighted the effectiveness of audio, video and modular instructions in teaching English subject.

Comparison of Pre-test and Post-test Mean Scores Analysis of the Three Groups in Mathematics Subject

Presented below in Table-18 are the mean and standard deviation of the pre-test and post-test scores of all the three groups and the calculated t-value.

Table-18: Mean and Standard Deviation of Pre-test and Post-test Scores of Control Group, Experimental Group Slow Learners and Normal Group Students and the Calculated t-values.

Name of Group	Pre-test			Post-test		Calculated
	N	M_1	$D.D_1$	M_2	$S.D_2$	t-value
Control Group	25	15.9	7.2	21.0	10.58	1.99@
Experimental Group	25	18.0	7.07	36.0	14.07	5.71**
Normal Group	25	48.3	16.6	51.9	16.2	0.78@

Note: @ Not Significant at 0.05 level.

** Significant at 0.01 level.

From Table-18, it is seen that the obtained t-values (1.99 and 0.78) in respect of control group and normal group are not significant whereas the t-value (5.71) obtained in respect of experimental group is significant. It indicates that the experimental group slow learners evinced significant variation in their post-test performance and their achievement in the post-test is higher than their achievement in the pre-test, whereas the control group slow learners and the normal group students could not make any significant difference in their post-test performance. Therefore, the formulated hypothesis that there exists significant difference between the pre-test and post-test mean scores of experimental group slow learners in mathematics subject is accepted.

Further, a comparative study of mean values obtained in respect of all the three groups brings to light the effectiveness of multimedia based modular approach in teaching mathematics to slow learners. In terms of per centage, the rate of progress made by the control group slow learners is 32% and the rate of progress made by the normal group students is 7.45%. But, the rate of progress made by the experimental group slow learners is 100% because they could double their mean score in the post-test. The vertical progress made by the experimental group slow learners bears testimony to the effectiveness of multimedia based modular approach in teaching mathematics to slow learners.

The above analysis gives the conclusion that there is significant difference between the pre-test and post-test mean scores of experimental group slow learners and their achievement in the post-test is higher than their achievement in the pre-test. Moreover, the rate of progress made by the experimental group slow learners is more than the rates of progress made by the other two groups. It also implies that multimedia based modular approach is more effective than the traditional lecture method in teaching mathematics to slow learners. Also, it conforms to the findings of Schram (1965), Maria Araselvi (1996) and Reddy and Ramar (1995) who have signified the effectiveness of video and modular instructions in teaching mathematics subject.

Comparison of Pre-test and Post-test Mean Scores Analysis of all the Three Groups in Science Subject

Table-19 depicts the mean and standard deviation of the pre-test and post-test scores of all the three groups and the calculated t-values.

Table-19: Mean and Standard Deviation of Pre-test and Post-test Scores of control Group, Experimental Group and the Normal Group and the Calculated t-values.

Name of Group	Pre-test			Post-test		Calculated
	N	M_1	$D.D_1$	M_2	$S.D_2$	t-value
Control Group	25	26.7	9.93	29.5	10.19	0.98@
Experimental Group	25	25.6	7.6	69.4	16.28	12.2**
Normal Group	25	52.3	13.48	58.3	7.84	1.92@

Note: @ Not Significant at 0.05 level.

**. Significant at 0.01 level.

From Table-19, it is understood that the obtained t-values (0.98 and 1.92) in respect of control group and normal group are not significant whereas the t-value (12.2) obtained in respect of experimental group is significant. It discloses that the experimental group slow learners showed significant and tremendous progress in their post-test performance and their achievement is higher in the post-test than in the pre-test, whereas the control group slow learners and the normal group students could not make any significant progress in their post-test performance. So, the formulated hypothesis that there exists significant difference between the pre-test and post-test mean scores of experimental group slow learners in science subject is accepted.

Further, a critical scrutiny of the mean values obtained in respect of all the three groups very much highlights the effectiveness of multimedia based modular approach in teaching science to slow learners. In terms of per centage, the rate of progress made by the control group slow learners is 10.4% and the rate of progress made by the normal group students is 11.4%. But, the rate of progress made by the experimental group slow learners is 171%. It is so because they could make a tremendous mean gain of 43.8 by increasing the score from a meagre mean of 25.6 in the pre-test to an astounding mean of 69.4 in the post-test.

It is surprising to note that the experimental group slow learners have excelled the normal group students in their post-test performance in science subject. The vertical progress made by the experimental group slow learners in the science post-test by their excellent performance avers the effectiveness of multimedia based modular approach in teaching science to slow learners and it also vouchsafes the advantage of multimedia based modular approach over the traditional lecture method.

From the above, it is concluded that there is significant difference between the pre-test and post-test mean scores of experimental group slow learners and their achievement is higher in the post-test than in the pre-test. Moreover, the rate of progress made by the experimental group slow learners is higher than the rate of progress made by the other two groups. Also, it is in the science post-test that the experimental group slow learners have surpassed even the normal group students. This performance par excellence of the experimental group slow learners signifies the effectiveness of multimedia based modular approach in teaching science to slow learners and it also testifies to the advantage of multimedia based modular approach over the traditional lecture method in teaching science to slow learners. Also, it supports the findings of Sinnathambi (1991), Madhur Gupta (1989), Basu (1981), Desai (1985), Schram (1965), Chelladurai (1994), Hopper (1992), Thalaimalai (1996) and Reddy and Ramar (1995) who have vouchsafed that video and modular instructions significantly improved the achievement of students in science after the experimental treatment.

Comparison of Pre-test and Post-test Mean Scores Analysis of all the three Groups in Social Science Subject

Mean, standard deviation of the pre-test and post-test scores of all the three groups and the calculated t-values are presented in Table-20.

Table-20: Mean and Standard Deviation of Pre-test and Post-test Scores of Control Group, Experimental Group and Normal Group and the Calculated t-values.

	Pre-test			Post-test		Calculated
Name of Group	N	M_1	$D.D_1$	M_2	$S.D_2$	t-value
Control Group	25	18.3	6.02	21.1	8.98	1.29@
Experimental Group	25	21.6	9.5	50.4	13.2	8.86**
Normal Group	25	52.3	10.4	54.3	11.07	0.66@

Note: @ Not Significant at 0.05 level.

** Significant at 0.01 level.

From Table 20, it is observed that the obtained t-values (11.29 and 0.66) in respect of control group and normal group respectively are not significant, whereas the t-value ((8.86) obtained in respect of experimental group is significant. It indicates that the experimental group slow learners evinced significant progress in their post-test performance and their achievement is higher in the post-test than in the pre-test, whereas the control group slow learners and the normal group students could not make any significant progress in their post-test performance. Hence, the formulated hypothesis that there exists significant difference between the pre-test and post-test mean scores of experimental group slow learners in social science subject is accepted.

Further, a comparative study of the mean values obtained in respect of all the three groups discloses the effectiveness of multimedia based modular approach in teaching social science to slow learners. Both the control group and normal group made a meagre mean gain of 2.8 and 2.3 while the experimental group slow learners could make a significant mean gain of 28.8. Even the difference made is more than their pre-test score. The rates of progress made by all the three groups *i.e.*, control, experimental and normal groups in terms of per centage are 15.3, 133 and 3.8 respectively. The rate of progress made by the experimental group slow learners vouches for the effectiveness of multimedia based modular approach in teaching social science to slow learners.

The above analysis gives the conclusion that there is significant difference between the pre-test and post-test mean scores of experimental group slow learners and their achievement is higher in the post-test than in the pre-test. Besides, the rate of progress shown by the experimental group slow learners is higher than the rates of progress made by the other two groups. The vertical variation in the experimental group slow learners' post-test performance is a sufficient indication to substantiate the effectiveness of multimedia based modular approach in teaching social science to slow learners. It conforms to the findings of Dhamija (1986) Mahange (1991) and Reddy and Ramar (1995) who have substantiated the effectiveness of modular instruction in teaching social science to normal students as well as backward students.

Comparison of Post-test Mean Scores Analysis of Experimental Group Slow Learners in Different Subjects

Table-21, depicts mean and standard deviation of the pre-test and post-test scores of experimental group slow learners in respect of each subject and the calculated t-values.

Table-21: Mean and Standard Deviation of Pre-test and Post-test Scores of Experimental Group Slow Learners for each Subject and the Calculated t-values.

Name of Group	Pre-test			Post-test		Calculated
	N	M_1	$D.D_1$	M_2	$S.D_2$	t-value
English	25	18.6	5.35	30.2	9.8	5.2 **
Mathematics	25	18.0	7.07	36.0	14.07	5.71 **
Science	25	25.6	7.60	69.4	16.28	12.2**
Social Science	25	21.6	9.5	50.4	13.2	8.86 **

Note: ** Significant at 0.01 level.

From Table-21, it is seen that the t-value obtained in respect of each subject is significant. But the degree of significance of difference differs from subject to subject. The t-values indicate that the post-test performance of the experimental group slow learners is better than their pre-test performance in respect of all the subjects. But the rate of progress made by them varies from subject to subject. Hence, the formulated hypothesis that the relative effectiveness of multimedia based modular approach differs from subject to subject is accepted.

A critical scan of the t-values discloses the degree of significance of difference among different subjects. The degree of significance of difference is highest in science (12.2) which is followed by social science with a t-value of 8.86. Trailing behind these two subjects are maths and English with t-values of 5.71 and 5.2 respectively. The obtained t-values are significant at 0.01 level for all the subjects. It is a true testimony to the effectiveness of multimedia based moduiar approach.

From the above, it is concluded that the relative effectiveness of multimedia based modular approach differs from subject to subject. The highest significant difference is found in science subject with a tremendous mean gain of 43.8 and 171% rate of progress. It is closely followed by social science subject with a mean gain of 28.8 and 133% rate of progress. Trailing behind these two subjects are mathematics and English which have mean gains of 18 and 11.6 and 100% and 64.4% rates of progress respectively. The very fact that the slow learners, who had hitherto no pass mean score in any subject, could now attain pass mean scores in three subjects, is a clear proof beyond doubt for the effectiveness of multimedia based modular approach with special reference to slow learner.

In terms of media effectiveness, the media effectiveness is more for science subject. The nature of science subject is such that it lends itself for concrete presentation and direct experience in the forms of project work and practicum in the modules. Then comes social science, where the project work and practicum have a bearing on students' achievement. This brings to light the fact that media effectiveness largely depends on the nature of the subject.

English demands active participation of students for a rapid learning. But in this approach, the media are quite active while the students are passive. Also, they need more exposure to true life situations for interaction. The present rate of progress also may be attributed to the interaction ensured in the practicum and project work of the module. Mathematics is a complex subject dealing with abstract concepts. It requires problem solving skill on the part of the learners. Though the multimedia based modular approach could enable the slow learners to show a significant increase in the post-test performance in mathematics, it could not bring about the same rate of progress as in science and social science subjects. Hence English and mathematics, which are complex and hard in nature, naturally trail behind.

An Overall Critical Analysis of the Results

An overall analysis reveals the following:

1. There is no significant difference in the pre-test performance between the control group slow learners

and the experimental group slow learners. The absence of variation in their pre-test performance bears testimony to the fact that both the control group and the experimental group in the present study were matched ones before the experiment.

2. There is no significant difference between the pre-test performance of control group slow learners and the normal group students. Further, the achievement of normal group students is higher than the achievement of control group slow learners.

3. There is significant difference between the pre-test mean scores of the experimental group slow learners and the normal group students. Further, the achievement of normal group students is higher than the achievement of experimental group slow learners.

4. There is no significant difference between the pre-test and post-test mean scores of the control group slow learners taught through traditional lecture method. Though their performance was better in the post-test, they could not make any significant difference.

5. There is significant difference between the pre-test and post-test scores of experimental group slow learners when the subjects are taught through the multimedia based modular approach. Further, their achievement is higher in the post-test than in the pre-test. Moreover, an analysis of rate of progress made by both control group slow learners and the experimental group slow learners throws light on the effectiveness of multimedia based modular approach with special reference to slow learners. From a meagre mean score of 20.6 in the pre-test, the experimental group slow learners could gain an impressive mean score of 46.2 in the post-test which is more than double the pre-test mean score. But, the control group slow learners could not make significant mean gain. This vouchsafes the advantage of multimedia based modular approach over the traditional lecture method. It conforms to the findings of Gabriel, Pillai and Gnanam (1989), Ramar (1994), Postlethwat, Novah

and Murray (1964), Rajaguru (1994) and Schmidt (1991) who all have established that multimedia and modular approach significantly enhanced the achievement of backward students such as low achievers and slow learners after the experimental treatment.

6. There is no significant difference between the pre-test and post-test scores of normal group students when taught through traditional lecture method. As in the case of control group, the normal group students also could not make any significant difference in their post-test performance because they could make a mean gain of 4.2 only for 47.

7. There is significant difference between the post-test scores of control group slow learners taught through traditional lecture method and the experimental group slow learners taught through multimedia based modular approach. Further, the achievement of the experimental group slow learners is higher than the achievement of control group slow learners. In terms of per centage, the rate of progress shown by the experimental group slow learners taught through multimedia based modular approach is 124% (from 20.6 to 46.2) (ref. Table-5), while the rate of progress made by the control group slow learners is 15% (from 19.8 to 22.8) (ref. Table-4). The variation in the rates of progress made by both the groups is the resultant product of multimedia based modular approach and it vouches for the effectiveness of multimedia based modular approach.

8. There is significant difference between the post-test scores of the slow learning boys and the slow learning girls in the control group taught through traditional lecture method. From the very meagre mean gain, (from 18 to 20.5) made by the slow learning girls in the control group, it is explicit that they could not make as much mean gain as the slow learning boys who made a mean gain of 4 from 20.3 to 24.3. This avers that the traditional lecture method is not effective to the slow learning girls and they need all the more a newer innovative method

of instruction to show significant difference in their performance.

9. Sex has not influenced the post-test performance of the experimental group slow learners as there exists no significant difference between the post-test scores of slow learning boys and slow learning girls in the experimental group. While the girls in the matched control group trailed behind the boys, the girls in the experimental group were at par with boys in the post-test performance. This may be attributed to the effectiveness of multimedia based modular approach.

10. There is significant difference between the post-test scores of the control group slow learners and the normal group students. Further, the achievement of the normal group students is higher than the achievement of control group slow learners. The mean values (19.8 and 22.8) obtained by the control group slow learners reveal that though they have made a progress by traditional lecture method, they could not narrow down the gap between them and the normal group students. It means that the traditional lecture method could not enable the control group slow learners to cope with normal students.

11. There is significant difference between the post-test scores of the experimental group slow learners and the normal group students. The achievement of normal group students is higher than the achievement of experimental group slow learners. However, a critical analysis of mean values signifies that the experimental group slow learners significantly improved their achievement after the experiment Moreover, the multimedia based modular approach enabled the experimental group slow learners to cope with the normal students to a great extent. The narrowed down gulf of difference between both the groups bears testimony to the effectiveness of multimedia based modular approach. Further, a comparative study of Table-10 and Table-11 testifies to the advantage of multimedia based modular approach over the traditional lecture method. It is in agreement with the findings of Schmidt (1991), Leitner (1992), Ramar (1994), Reddy

and Ramar (1994,1995) and Postlethwat (1964) who have substantiated that CAI, video instruction and modular instructions could enable the backward students like low achievers and slow learners to cope with normal students taught through traditional lecture method.

12. There is no significant difference in the achievements of control group slow learners between the post-test and retention test. It is observed that the mean value has decreased by 0.4. It indicates that the control group slow learners could not remember at the time of retention test all the facts and figures they were aware of at the time of post-test. This can be ascribed for the decreased mean value in the retention test. The post-test score is higher than the retention test score in respect of most of the control group slow learners. The mean values of post-test and retention test further suggest that the traditional lecture method could neither contribute to nor promote retention.

13. There is significant difference between the post-test performance and retention test performance of experimental group slow learners. However, the significant mean difference (25.6) between the pre-test and post-test scores of experimental group slow learners highlights the volume of new additional informations acquired by them at the time of post-test. This fast learnt informations could be properly processed in their minds and kept in memory storage even after a period of two months without loss or distortion. This is well testified by the fact that the experimental group slow learners could improve upon their post-test performance in the retention test. Further, it substantiates that the multimedia based modular approach could contribute to and promote retention of slow learners. The better retention of experimental group slow learners is the resultant product of multimedia based modular treatment given to them during the period of experimentation. Also, it strengthens the findings of Hopper (1982) and Rajaguru (1994), Oberai (1981) and Kumar (1981) who have established that multimedia

strategy and modular approach very much promote the retention of the students.

14. There is significant difference in the achievements of the normal group students between the post-test and retention test. It is noticed that the mean value has decreased by 0.8. It also indicates that whatever informations they had in their minds at the time of post-test could not be recalled without loss or distortion at the time of retention test. This can be ascribed for their decreased mean value in the retention test. The post-test score is higher than the retention test score for most of the normal group students. A critical study of the mean values of the post-test and retention test further signifies that the traditional lecture method could neither promote nor facilitate transfer or recall.
15. There is significant difference between the retention test scores of the slow learning boys and the slow learning girls in the control group. The achievement of slow learning boys is higher than the achievement of slow learning girls. The difference that was present in the post-test persisted in the retention test also.
16. There exists no significant difference between the retention test scores of slow learning boys and slow learning girls in the experimental group. Both the boys and girls in experimental group have evinced same degree of retention by recalling the facts and concepts already learnt till the post-test at the time of retention test. The overcrowding of facts and concepts and the rapid acquisition of new informations and concepts during the period of experimentation did not affect their memory storage and retention. The very fact that the slow learners, who are known to be slow to "catch on", have been able to acquire this much of information in a short period and they have been able to retain them in memory for a considerable time, testifies to the effectiveness of multimedia based modular approach. It supports the findings of Madhur Gupta (1989), Oberai (1981), Kumar (1981) and Rajaguru (1994) who have

established that multimedia instructional strategy promotes retention of the students.

17. There is significant difference between the pre-test and post-test scores of the experimental group slow learners in English subject. Their achievement is higher in the post-test, than in the pre-test. Moreover, the rate of progress made by the experimental group students is higher than the rates of progress made by the other two group students. This fact asseverates the effectiveness of multimedia based modular treatment. It is in agreement with the findings of George (1966), Kumar (1981), Kasinathan (1992), Ramar (1994) and Natarajan (1996) who have highlighted the effectiveness of audio, video and modular instructions in teaching English subject.

18. There exists significant difference between the pre-test and post-test scores of experimental group slow learners in mathematics subject and their achievement is higher in the post test than in the pre-test. Moreover, the rate of progress made by the experimental group slow learners is more than the rates of progress made by the other two groups. It also implies that multimedia based modular approach is more effective than the traditional lecture method in teaching mathematics to slow learners. Also, it conforms to the findings of Schram (1965), Maria Araselvi (1996) and Reddy and Ramar (1995) who have signified the effectiveness of video and modular instructions in teaching mathematics subject.

19. There is significant difference between the pre-test and post-test scores of experimental group slow learners in science subject and their achievement is higher in the post-test than in the pre-test. Moreover, the rate of progress made by the experimental group slow learners is higher than the rates of progress made by the other two groups. Also, it is in the science post-test that the experimental group slow learners have surpassed even the normal group students. This performance par excellence of the experimental group slow learners

signifies the effectiveness of multimedia modular approach in teaching science to slow learners and also it testifies to the advantage of multimedia based modular approach over the traditional lecture method in teaching science to slow learners. Also, it supports the findings of Sinnathambi (1991), Madhur Gupta (1989), Basu (1981), Desai (1985), Schram (1965), Chelladurai (1994), Hopper (1992), Thalaimalai (1996) and Reddy and Ramar (1995) who have vouchsafed that video and modular instructions significantly improved the achievement of students in science after the experimental treatment.

20. There exists significant difference between the pre-test and post-test scores of the experimental group slow learners and their achievement is higher in the post-test than in the pre-test. Besides, the rate of progress made by the experimental group slow learners is more than the rates of progress made by the other two groups. The vertical variation in the experimental group slow learners' post-test performance is a sufficient indication to substantiate the effectiveness of multimedia based modular approach in teaching social science to slow learners. It conforms to the findings of Dhamija (1986) Mahange (1991) and Reddy and Ramar (1995) who have substantiated the effectiveness of modular instruction in teaching social science to normal students as well as backward students.

21. There are significant differences between the pre-test and post-test scores of experimental group slow learners in respect of all the subjects. The highest significant difference is found in science subject with a tremendous mean gain of 43.8 and 171% rate of progress. It is closely followed by social science subject with a mean gain of 28.8 and 133% rate of progress. Trailing behind these two subjects are mathematics and English which have mean gains of 18 and 11.6 and 100% and 64.4% rates of progress respectively. The very fact that the slow learners, who had hitherto no pass mean score in any subject, could now attain pass mean scores in three subjects, is a clear proof, beyond doubt, for the

effectiveness of multimedia based modular approach with special reference to slow learners.

In terms of media effectiveness, the media effectiveness is more for science subject. The nature of science subject is such that it lends itself for concrete presentation and direct experience in the forms of project work and practicum in the modules. Then comes social science, where the project work and practicum have a bearing on students' achievement. This brings to light the fact that media effectiveness largely depends on the nature of the subject.

English demands active participation of students for a rapid learning. But in this approach, the media are quite active while the students are passive. Also, they need more exposure to true life situations for interaction. The present rate of progress also may be attributed to the interaction ensured in the practicum and project work of the module. Mathematics is a complex subject dealing with abstract concepts. It requires problem solving skill on the part of the learners. Though the multimedia based modular approach could enable the slow learners to show a significant increase in the post-test performance in mathematics, it could not bring about the same rates of progress as in science and social science subjects. Hence, Mathematics and English, which are complex and hard in nature, naturally trail behind.

Summary and suggestions are presented in the succeeding chapter.

6

SUMMARY AND SUGGESTION

SUMMARY

The research work carried out by the investigator, and the findings arrived at are summed up in this chapter under appropriate headings along with limitations, implications of the study and suggestions made for further research.

Introduction

The problem that plagues every teacher in every subject at every grade level of educational system is how to teach one lesson to a class that contains students with different skills and learning rates. Accommodating instruction to student differences is one of the most fundamental problems and the foremost task of an educator. The problem of accommodating student differences is so important that many educators have suggested that instruction be completely individualised so that student can work independently at their own rates. Therefore the task becomes one of developing the work of the school in response to pupil diversity. Ainscow (1997) notes that this has to include a consideration of overall organisation, curriculum and classroom practice, and support for learning and staff development. There is an increasing amount of evidence from various countries suggesting that measures schools take to cater for pupil diversity can lead to more effective form of education for the pupils.

Ainscow and Hart (1992) map out some possible perspectives on educational difficulties. These perspectives are attempts to characterise alternative ways of looking at the phenomenon of educational difficulty, based on different sets of assumptions that lead to different explanations, different frames of reference and different kinds of questions to be addressed. In this sense they lead to assumptions that provide the basis of different theoretical positions.

The first perspective seeks to explain educational difficulties in terms of the characteristics of individual pupils. This remains the dominant perspective in the special needs field, where the nature of educational difficulties is explained in terms of particular disabilities, social background and/or psychological attributes. The frame of reference created by this perspective is the individual child, and responses are chosen that seek to change or support the child in order to facilitate participation in the process of schooling. Traditionally responses have taken the form of removal of the child from the mainstream curriculum for specialist help. However, more recently, responses have begun to develop which allow help to be provided in the context of the regular classroom.

The second perspective explains educational difficulties in terms of a mismatch between the characteristics of particular children and the organisation and/or curriculum arrangements made for them. Here support may be directed towards helping the child to meet the demands and expectations of system, if this is assumed to be fixed or-for the time being at least-unchangeable. Or it may be directed towards making modifications to the system in order to extend the range of pupils that can be accommodated. In many respects current 'state of the art' responses (*e.g.,* whole-school approaches, differentiation) are informed by this perspective. Further, it is a perspective that is seen as arising as a result of dissatisfaction with the first perspective, which is seen as being a 'deficit model'.

The third perspective explains educational difficulties in terms of curriculum limitations, using the term curriculum in a broad sense to include all the planned and, indeed, unplanned experiences offered to pupils. Thus in this perspective there is a concern with what can be learnt from the difficulties experienced by some children about the limitations of provision currently made for all pupils. The assumption is that changes introduced for the benefit of those experiencing difficulties can improve learning for all children. Those adopting this perspective are critical of the limitations of an individual frame of reference, even where this is used to raise questions about the adequacy of curriculum organisation and practice as currently provided for individual pupils. They argue that a wider frame is needed, focusing on curriculum organisation and practice as currently provided for all pupils. The task involves continually seeking ways of improving overall conditions for learning, with difficulties acting as indicators of how improvements might be achieved (Ainscow, 1994). Those who adopt this perspective are likely to favour approaches that encourage enquiry as a means of achieving improvement, *e.g.,* various forms of partnership teaching, action research.

The above discussions lay a much greater emphasis on practitioner research in the special needs field so that greater understanding of how educational contexts can be developed in order to foster the learning of all the children in the classroom is most likely to emerge. Taking this view into consideration, an earnest attempt has been made in this experiment to design instruction so as to reach out to all learners especially the slow learners who are in the lowest rung of the ladder and constitute about a considerable per centage of student population in India.

The students who are generally unable to cope with the work normally expected of their age group are called slow learners. These students with less than I.Q. 90 are traditionally labelled "dull normal" and they are generally slower to "catch on" to whatever is being taught if it involves symbolic, abstract or conceptual subject matter. They lack concentration, retention and abstract thinking. As a result, they find it very difficult to keep up with their age group.

But, these slow learners constitute such a considerable per centage of student population that they can not be ignored.

Also, one can not conceive of any all round national development without ensuring adequate human resource development. Effective and optimum utilisation of other resources also depends on the degree of human resource development. Children of today are the citizens of tomorrow and they are going to be the pillars of this country. Hence, it is very essential to ensure that each pillar is as strong as the other. This warrants a special instructional strategy for the slow learners. Since education functions as the king-pin of national development, we have to ameliorate the learning process of slow learners also. This warrants a special instructional strategy for the slow learners. Multimedia based modular approach is such a strategy.

The traditional teacher depends on verbal exposition. But considerable visualisations of objects and process are essential for formulation of accurate concepts. What impact a visual presentation can do, any amount of verbal exposition can not do. An appropriate educational technology in the hands of a competent teacher can ensure better teaching learning process. Moreover, in a fast developing world where knowledge explosion is taking place in every sphere, it is unreasonable to expect that the spoken or written words alone could convey the volume of relevant information to the learner.

Television and record player are the powerful media which have become highly influential in the present day life style. They play a pivotal role in the teaching learning process also. Multimedia packages help to overcome barriers. They go beyond the four walls of the classrooms. It fulfills the gap in learning. Difficult processes can be shown with ease. Inaccessible places can be viewed sitting in the cosy classroom. These multimedia packages can penetrate more deeply into human character with an immediate excitement than any other single medium. The dual effect of audio and video strengthens and enriches the understanding and expedites the mastery of the concept.

Realising the importance of multi-media, the National Policy of Education (1986) emphasises that the modem educational technology, in general, should reach out to the most distant areas and the most depressed sections of beneficiaries.

Modules are self-contained and auto-instructional material dealing with a single conceptual unit. It caters to individual differences. Each student can take his own time to complete the module. Here, what matters much is the mastery of the subject, not the time. So these modules are very suitable to the slow learners. Moreover, when we provide multimedia base to the modules, they are more effective, especially to slow learners.

Vardhini (1983) developed and tried out "a multimedia instructional strategy for teaching science at secondary level" and found it to be more effective and also asserted that multimedia strategy can be implemented at school level without having to spend too much money or time. Basu (1981) studied "effectiveness of multimedia programmed instructional material in teaching of physics" and found that the strategy enabled the learners to reach the level of mastery learning.

According to Wattsen and Hill (1984), Video has proved to be one of the most popular advancements of the 1970's and 1980's. Video feedback increased the congruency between students' and teachers' perception of some aspects of public speaking performance (Broyles, 1986). Further, Andrews (1986) observed that Video feedback was significantly more effective than verbal feedback. Interactive video programme was found to be more effective for teacher's training (Kwan, 1986; Mclean, 1986). Helley (1987) reported that achievement of video subtitled group was significantly higher than that of the group subjected to textual video programme.

Interactive video programmes were found to be more effective in comparison to linear video programmes (Abrams, 1986), and Interactive video presentation took significantly less time than the lecture based presentation (Clark, 1987). Finally, video instructional material was found to be effective in terms of achievement and attitude of students towards 'advance organiser model' (James, 1988).

The live teaching of any subject calls for an extension of the students' visual experience and awareness. Television aided by its power of magnification can offer a close view of a scientific demonstration to any number of students. It can facilitate teaching of science and mathematics with animated diagrams and it can bring social science alive by filmed interviews and case studies of men and women in action in distant places.

Dhamija (1985) made a comparative study of the effectiveness of three approaches of instruction—conventional, radio vision and modular approach on achievement of students in social studies and found that modular approach was more effective in teaching of civics. Hopper W.A.F. (1982) conducted "an experimental study in the use of modular approach for teaching biology in standard XI' and found it to be more effective in terms of mean gain in cognitive achievement. Sahajahan (1980) conducted "an experimental study of teaching science in standards VI and VII through Modules' and found that the modular way of learning was more effective than the conventional method.

Ramar (1994) has established the effectiveness of multimedia based modular approach with reference to low achievers in std VIII. Reddy and Ramar, (1994, 1995 and 1996) have asserted the effectiveness of multimedia based modular approach in teaching science, maths, and social science respectively to the low achievers. They also found that the multimedia based modular approach could enable the low achievers to cope with normal students to a great extent.

Soundararaja Rao and Rajaguru (1995) have conducted studies on slow learners but not related to effectiveness of multimedia based modular approach. Research studies reveal that the multimedia treatment is more effective to backward students than to normal students. Hence, in this study an attempt is made to find out and measure the effectiveness of multimedia based modular approach in promoting the achievement of slow learners.

Title of the Problem

"EFFECTIVENESS OF MULTIMEDIA BASED MODULAR APPROACH WITH SPECIAL REFERENCE TO SLOW LEARNERS"

Objectives of the Study

The following are the objectives of the study:

1. To develop multimedia based modules for English, Maths, Science, and Social Science subjects of Std VIII.
2. To assess the achievement of slow learners in Std VIII when the subjects are taught through traditional lecture method.
3. To find out the achievement of slow learners in Std VIII when the subjects are taught through multimedia based modular approach.
4. To find out the achievement of normal students in Std VIII when the subjects are taught through traditional lecture method.
5. To find out whether there exists any significant difference between the pre-test mean scores of the control group slow learners and experimental group slow learners.
6. To assess whether there exists any significant difference between the pre-test mean scores of control group slow learners and the normal group students.
7. To find out whether there is any significant difference between the pre-test mean scores of experimental group slow learners and the normal group students.
8. To assess whether there exists any significant difference between the pre-test and post-test mean scores of control group slow learners when the subjects are taught through traditional lecture method.
9. To find out whether there is any significant difference between the pre-test and post-test mean scores of experimental group slow learners when the subjects are taught through multimedia based modular approach.
10. To assess whether there exists any significant difference between the pre test and post-test mean scores of normal group students taught through traditional lecture method.

11. To find out whether there is any significant difference between the post-test mean scores of the slow learners in the experimental group and the slow learners in the control group.

12. To assess whether there exists any significant difference between the post-test mean scores of the slow learning boys and the slow learning girls in the control group taught through traditional lecture method.

13. To find out whether there is any significant difference between the post-test mean scores of the slow learning boys and the slow learning girls in the experimental group taught through multimedia based modular approach.

14. To assess whether there exists any significant difference between the post-test mean scores of the slow learners in the control group and the students in the normal group.

15. To find out whether there is any significant difference between the post-test mean scores of the slow learners in the experimental group and the students in the normal group.

16. To assess whether there exists any significant difference between the post-test and retention test mean scores of the control group slow learners.

17. To find out whether there is any significant difference between the post-test and retention test mean scores of the slow learners in the experimental group.

18. To assess whether there exists any significant difference between the post-test and retention test mean scores of normal group students.

19. To assess whether there exists any significant difference between the retention test mean scores of the slow learning boys and slow learning girls in the control group.

20. To find out whether there is any significant difference between the retention test mean scores of the slow

learning boys and the slow learning girls in the experimental group.

21 To assess whether there exists any significant difference between the pre-test and post-test mean scores of the experimental group slow learners in English subject.

22 To find out whether there is any significant difference between the pre-test and post-test mean scores of the experimental group slow learners, in mathematics subject.

23. To assess whether there is any significant difference between the pre-test and post-test mean scores of the experimental group slow learners in science subject.

24. To find out whether there is any significant difference between the pre-test and post-test mean scores of the experimental group slow learners in social science subject.

25. To assess whether the relative effectiveness of multimedia modular approach differs from subject to subject selected for this study.

Hypotheses of the Study

Keeping in view the objectives of the study, the following hypotheses are formulated for testing:

1. There exists no significant difference between the pre-test mean scores of contr l group slow learners and experimental group slow learners.
2. There exists significant difference between the pre-test mean scores of control group slow learners and the normal group students.
3. There exists significant difference between the pre-test mean scores of experimental group slow learners and the normal group students.
4. There exists no significant difference between the pre-test and post-test mean scores of control group slow learners when the subjects are taught through traditional lecture method.

5. There exists significant difference between the pre-test and post-test mean scores of experimental group slow learners taught through multimedia based modular approach.

6. There exists no significant difference between the pre-test and post-test mean scores of normal group students taught through traditional lecture method.

7. There exists significant difference between the post-test mean scores of the slow learners in the experimental group and the slow learners in the control group.

8. There exists significant difference between the post-test mean scores of the slow learning boys and slow learning girls in the control group.

9. There is significant difference between the post-test mean scores of the slow learning boys and slow learning girls in the experimental group.

10. There exists significant difference between the post-test mean scores of the slow learners in the control group and the students in the normal group.

11. There exists no significant difference between the post-test mean scores of the slow learners in the experimental group and the students in the normal group.

12. There is no significant difference between the post-test and retention test mean scores of the control group slow learners.

13. There exists no significant difference between the post test and retention test mean scores of the slow learners in the experimental group.

14. There is no significant difference between the post-test and retention test mean scores of normal group students.

15. There exists significant difference between the retention test mean scores of the slow learning boys and the slow learning girls in the control group.

16. There exists significant difference between the retention test mean scores of the slow learning boys and slow learning girls in the experimental group.

17. There exists significant difference between the pre-test and post-test mean scores of the experimental group slow learners in English subject.
18. There exists significant difference between the pre-test and post-test mean scores of the experimental group slow learners in mathematics subject.
19. There exists significant difference between the pre-test and post-test mean scores of the experimental group slow learners in science subject.
20. There exists significant difference between the pre-test and post-test mean scores of the experimental group slow learners in social science subject.
21. Relative effectiveness of multimedia based modular approach differs from subject to subject.

Scope of the Study

Multimedia is a composite of auditory and visual presentation. It can reach audience of unlimited size. It can transmit programme content without delay from the point of origin to the point of reception. Keeping this view in mind, the primary focus of the study is to develop multimedia based modules for certain units in all the subjects of standard VIII, except Tamil. Four main constituents of multimedia are used in this study. They are:

1. Audio Cassettes.
2. Video Cassettes.
3. Software for computer assisted instruction.
4. Other HTIM and LTIM available in the school.

Audio cassettes procured from the International Educational Research Centre, New Delhi, and ACE Educational Systems Pvt. Ltd., Madras, which cover most of the units, are used in this study in addition to the audio cassettes developed by the researcher covering the left out units. The instructional presentation by the teacher was recorded so as to suit the slow learners.

Likewise, the video cassettes procured from the International Educational Research Centre, New Delhi were used to provide multimedia base to the modules relevant to the particular concepts. For those units for which ready made cassettes were not available, required multimedia packages were developed by the investigator himself.

In addition to the 'audio and video cassettes, computer software for computer assisted instruction was also prepared. The computer assisted instruction was programmed in such a way as to promote auto learning by the slow learner at his own pace. These multimedia packages were developed with the help of concerned technical experts and subject resource persons.

Apart from the audio and video cassettes procured from different agencies and developed by the investigator, other HTIM like microscope, microslides etc., and LTIM such as colour charts, models both working and non working etc., were also used as an integral part of multimedia based modules.

Modules of all the units were given to the experimental group slow learners in the form of a Handbook so as to facilitate auto learning by the slow learners at their own pace. Teacher support system was limited to the extent of operating the multimedia packages, clarifying doubts and guiding the project works.

Three units were selected for each subject for the purpose of developing and measuring the effectiveness of multimedia based modules. Each unit was divided into two to four conceptual sub-units. For mathematics equations and Inequations, cubo and cuboid and circular ring were selected for study. For science one unit from physics *i.e.*, magnetism, one unit from chemistry *i.e.*, compounds of carbon and another unit from biology *i.e.*, cellular organisation were included in the study. For social science subject, one unit from history *i.e.*, religious and social reformations, one unit from civics *i.e.*, defence organisations in India and one more unit from geography *i.e.*, Indian forests and wildlife were earmarked for the study. For English, since language plays a more prominent role than the subject matter, sentence pattern and non-finite verbs and spoken English covering pure vowels, diphthongs and consonants were earmarked for preparation of modules.

Fifty slow learners of S.S.H.N. Higher Secondary School, Muhavoor were selected for the study. Twenty five of them constituted the experimental group while the rest formed the control group. The main focus of the study is to measure the effectiveness and advantage of multimedia based modular approach over the traditional lecture method in promoting the achievement of the slow learners in standard VIII. In addition to the pre-test and post-test, a retention test was also conducted to assess the impact of multimedia based modular approach on the retention of the slow learners. Finally, the study also aims to measure the extent to which the multimedia based modular approach enables the slow learners to cope with normal students. For this purpose, a normal group was also constituted comprising twenty five average and above average students selected from the population, from which the sample for the study was drawn.

Need and Importance of the Study

Need and importance of the study can be classified from two different angles as need from media point of view and need from slow learners point of view.

Need from Media Point of View

Teaching effectively is the most important of all the competencies required of a successful teacher. Since effective teaching deals with the needs, interest and abilities of pupils as individuals, it requires knowledge of the environment in which the pupil lives, the development problem he or she faces and his/her mental abilities. It is more true so when the teacher is dealing with the slow learners. It also calls for an understanding of the learning processes essential for creating an environment where learning can take place and for making instruction so stimulating that every pupil will be motivated to learn. Stimulating pupils to think critically, independently and creatively is essential for effective teaching.

Effective teaching in any subject depends largely upon the introduction of newer methods of instruction. There is a growing need for trying out newer methods of instruction and establishing their effectiveness in teaching. Now-a-days a teacher cannot depend on any single method of teaching. The teacher has to try out several innovative methods to present the content to the students. When they are taught by innovative methods, the students are able to understand the concept, principles and content in an effective manner.

The immense knowledge explosion taking place in the world warrants newer methods of teaching. Students need unique experience in the presentation of the content. Multimedia based modular approach provides such unique experience to students. But, utmost care should be evinced in development of modules and multimedia packages which is a complex technical work.

Destiny of a nation is being shaped in her classrooms. The growing number of slow learners at all levels of our educational system warrants such a study, as this proposed one, to be undertaken for the enrichment of our teaching learning process.

Above all, human resource development should be at the focus of any research effort for a developing country like India which has abundant human resources In the Indian system of education, it is observed that the human resources-teachers and learners, are under developed and perform less than their capabilities. The learners are under developed in the sense that they are not achieving in tune with their capabilities. Even some of the most efficient teachers are not adequately equipped to identify and guide the under achievers and slow learners to reach their optimum levels. As a result, the institutions in turn are not able to send their products into the society as fully developed learners. To ensure this we need a different strategy which can cater to individual differences. Multimedia based modular approach is such a strategy.

Although, much has been achieved in this field of education, there are many opportunities for experiment and research. Throughout we have been constantly aware of the need for further investigation of the learning, thinking and adjustment of slow learning children so that teaching method can be precisely planned to suit their needs (Tansley and Gulliford, 1962).

Now, the current trend is propagating auto learning by the learner himself at his own pace. This paved the way for CAI, CAL, etc., Here the teacher is merely a facilitator of learning. He need not suffocate the learners with all the informations at a time. In auto learning, the learner can take his own time and he can proceed at his own pace till he completes the lesson. It is not the time but mastery learning which is the governing criterion here. This is where the multimedia based modular approach exactly fits in.

Multimedia learning experiences represent a natural way for learning to take place. Learning can be accelerated by involving maximum number of senses. Sensory experience forms the foundation of intellectual activity within any formal school situation and learners differ in the effectiveness of their sense reception. Multimedia learning experiences have the advantage of appealing to the individual, the learner's pace, interest and readiness.

Besides, cognition and conceptualisation depend on a chain of events which begin with the learner's perception of stimulus, be the auditory, visual, tactile and olfactory. It is important that these initial learning experiences be accurate, dependable and understandable. Unless the learner's initial sensory impressions are accurate, it will be impossible for them to have reliable conceptualisation and understandings. With the existing numerous kinds of aids, carefully organised presentation of information through a variety of media should occupy the learner's conscious attention to living stimuli (Mohan & Rajeswari, 1995). This is what is precisely ensured by the multimedia based modular approach.

Multimedia based modules help to stimulate interest in learning. It economises time and effort, reduces verbalism in teaching and imparts broad education to pupils. Not only children but also adults remember facts better when the multimedia aids are used to explain the concepts. Further multimedia based modular approach supports Paivio's (1971) dual code theory of memory which suggests that information coded both visually and verbally is remembered better than information coded in only one of those two ways.

Instructors sometimes consider it difficult or impossible to individualise learning while carrying on group instruction. But opportunities do exist to individualise learning with group of nearly any size (James Brown *et al.*, 1985). To do so requires systematic planning and creative uses of media sources as in modularisation.

Need from Slow Learners Point of View

The slow learners lack concentration. So they can not concentrate on the instructional presentation for or more than 45 minutes. In multimedia based modular approach a single unit is divided into three to four conceptual sub units. Each sub unit constitutes the subject content for development of one module. The duration of each module is 20 to 25 minutes only. So the slow learners will be able to concentrate on the concept. Also, it caters to the short span of attention of the slow learners.

A learning module is a self contained and self-instructional package dealing with a single conceptual unit or subject matter. It can be used in any setting, convenient to the learner and the learner can complete the module at his own pace. It may be used individually or in small learning groups. In this way multimedia based modular approach accommodates instruction to individual differences. Here what matters most is the mastery of the subject, not the time. So the modules are very suitable to the students and they are more effective for slow learners.

One of the most frequent complaints about slow learners is the weakness of their memory. Of all the problems that hamper educational progress, the most frequent is a weakness in what may be termed long-term memory. Slow learners need to go over the material more times before it is fixed in their mind, and more frequent revision is required to prevent forgetting. The efficiency of the initial learning is important as well as actual retention and recall. Multimedia based modular approach takes care of these problems by providing frequent revision and repetition in each module.

The slow learners are very poor in abstract thinking. It is because they are unable to understand the relationship between things. They are slower to perceive and use possible association.

Meaningful associations are of great importance not only for comprehension but also for prolonged retention. The learning materials presented in the module for each objective, the project work and the practicum incorporated in the learning module enable the slow learners to surmount the problem of abstract thinking, and to understand the possible association which will, ultimately, tell upon their retention.

It is a fallacy to think that just because the slow learners are limited in intelligence, they can only learn by rote memorisation. They also can make meaningful learning where there is concrete presentation of subject matter. Slow learners must understand as much as they can of what they are learning; and then they need more repetition, revision and practice to ensure retention. Multi-media based modular approach takes care of concrete presentation of subject matter by incorporating necessary diagrams, sketches, pictures, worksheets, examples, dimensional drawings etc., with the learning material at appropriate places. Also, modular approach provides for the required review, repetition, and revision by highlighting the main points in learning materials, various tests and in recapitulation and summary. It provides for practice in project work and practicum. Thus, in many ways, the multimedia based modular approach proves to be suitable for slow learners. Hence, to establish the effectiveness of multi-media based modules with special reference to slow learners a study of this sort is warranted.

Dhamija (1985), Hopper (1982), Sahajahan (1980), Ramar (1994), Chelladurai (1994) and Natarajan (1996) have conducted experimental studies on the effectiveness of modular approach. Ramar (1994), Lokanadha Reddy and Ramar (1994, 1995 and 1996) have conducted experimental studies on the effectiveness of multimedia based modular approach. Soundararaja Rao and Rajaguru (1995) have conducted studies on slow learners but not related to effectiveness of modular approach.

Systematic researches are, therefore, necessary to develop modules so as to assess their effectiveness with special reference to slow learners. Also, we can not afford to ignore the slow learners who constitute a sizable portion of student population.

The present study is an attempt to develop modules for all the subjects of std VIII except Tamil for the use of slow learners studying in std VIII and to measure their effectiveness and also to assess their advantage over the traditional lecture method.

Methodology

The various steps followed in the methodology of this study are development of modules and multimedia packages for all the subjects of std VIII except Tamil, construction of research tools, identifying slow learners, sampling technique, design of the study, administration of tool for pre-test, post-test and retention test and employing appropriate statistical techniques for arriving at scientific conclusions.

Development of Modules

The major objective of the study was to develop modules for all the subjects of std VIII. In the development of modules, the guidelines given by the NCERT have been followed, by the investigator. In English, since learning of English language items is more important than learning the subject matter of prose and poetry, sentence pattern, non-finite verbs and vowels and consonants were chosen for the purpose of developing modules and experimentation. In mathematics three units *i.e.*, equation, inequations, circular ring, cubes and cuboids were included for investigations. In science, one unit from physics *i.e.*, magnetism, one unit from chemistry *i.e.*, compounds of carbon and one unit from biology *i.e.*, cellular organisation were chosen for development of modules and experimentation. In social science, one unit from history *i.e.*, religious and social reformations in India, one unit from civics *i.e.*, defence organisation in India and one unit from geography *i.e.*, Indian forests and wild life were selected for the purpose of this study. Each of the above units was divided into three to four conceptual sub-units. Each sub-unit constituted the subject content for development of one module.

Each module was developed in self-contained and self-instructional manner. Each has at its first page the overview of the module which specified the unit, the conceptual sub-unit and the pattern of the module. In the succeeding page instruction is given to the students as to how to use the modules for self learning. The third page contains the entry test consisting of objective type test items to assess the preliminary knowledge or the entering behaviour of the students required for learning the module. Then comes the pre-test which helps to self evaluate the student's status when he proceeds with the module. After the pre-test, general and specific objectives are delineated in behavioural terms. Next, the learning materials for objectives I and II are presented. Provision is made for formative evaluation in the form of embedded tests. Summative evaluation can be made in the post-test. In each module provision has been made for practicum and projects to be undertaken as follow up work. For students' guidance a list of reference books and keys to all the tests are furnished at the end.

The above provisions enable the students to make self study with the help of the modules. The modules thus developed were then subjected to individual and group try outs and necessary correction, modification, refinements etc. were made in the modules. Both the try outs ensured better refinement and perfection of modules. The agreement of views of experts who reviewed the modules, was taken as the index of validity of the content of the modules. After this validation, the modules were made ready for the use of slow learners.

Development of Multimedia Packages

After developing the modules, the investigator had to shoulder the Herculean task of providing multimedia base to the prepared modules. Every possible effort was taken to develop LTIM for each module. It ranged from colour chart to Thermocol Model. The list of LTIM and HTIM used in this study are given in Appendix-II. Eight video cassettes had been procured from the International Educational Research Centre, New Delhi for this purpose before hand. Those cassettes were played to the slow learners during the period of experimentation. For maths, one cassette on "equations" and another on "cubes", for science two cassettes on "chromosomes", one cassette on "photosynthesis", two cassettes on "science experiments" and one cassette on magnetism were purchased. Audio cassettes were also bought from Madras. Even then all the units could not be covered. So, there was need to develop video and audio cassettes by the researcher himself to provide multimedia base to the developed modules.

Though the audio and the video cassettes were played to the slow learners as and when required, to maintain logical sequence, they were recorded in proper sequential order. For the units not covered by the readymade audio-video cassettes, the investigator had to resort to video shooting and editing. Outstanding teachers of meritorious service were selected for this purpose to present the modular lesson as per the instructional direction of the investigator. A professional videographer was employed for shooting. The shooting was done in the classroom of the school where the experiment was carried out. It took some ten days to accomplish the task. The shots were made according to the description of the scenes such as Long Shot (L.S.) Medium Shot (M.S.) Close-up Shot (C.S.) Zoom In (ZI) and Zoom Out (ZO).

After proper editing and validation, the video cassettes were made ready for instructional presentation to the experimental group slow learners. In similar manner, audio cassettes were also prepared for the units not covered by the ready made cassettes and they were subjected to proper validation before handing over to the experimental group slow learners for their use during experimentation.

Since a multimedia approach would be incomplete without application of computer software, a CAI software covering the units selected for the study, was developed with the help of computer experts. Once the programming was over, it was subjected to try-outs. In the try-outs the students expressed that it was more conducive for learning at their own pace. Also, they found it more effective since the interaction with the computer had a motivating quality of its own. After validation, the CAI software was made ready for the use of experimental group slow learners.

Identifying Slow Learners

For the purpose of this investigation the slow learners were identified on the basis of a three phase process. The phases are:

(i) Identifying phase,

(ii) Scientific confirmatory phase,

(iii) Counter-check phase,

For the first phase, the third measure recommended by Tansley and Gulliford (1962) which incorporates first, second and fourth measures of Chintamani Kar (1982) was followed. In the second phase, the identified slow learners were subjected to a scientific confirmatory test. For this purpose, Standard Progressive Matrices designed by Raven J.C. and successfully and effectively used by Soundararaja Rao and Rajaguru (1995) in Indian setting was administered to them as a scientific confirmatory test. In the confirmatory test, those who got less score (9-15/60 or below 25th per centile point) and took more time, were classified as slow learners. Lastly, these slow learners were counter-checked on the basis of their rate of learning as suggested by Kirk (1972).

Construction of Tool

To measure the performance of the students before and after the experiment, an achievement test was constructed by the investigator on the basis of item analysis. Out of 120 objective type items, 100 items were finally selected on the basis of item analysis for the final form of the achievement test. With regard to item difficulty, the per centage clustered around the 50 per cent level in most cases. On the basis of this analysis, too easy and too difficult test items were deleted in the final form of achievement test. As for test item discriminating power, 50 per cent of the test items had D-value exceeding +0.40, less than 40 per cent had D values between +0.40 and +0.20, Also about 10 per cent had D values between +0.20 and 0.0 and such test items were excluded from the final form of achievement test. The final form of achievement test is given in Appendix IV.

Each item was scored 'one' mark for the correct response and 'zero' for the wrong response. The duration of the test was

2 hours. The same achievement test was used as pre-test, post-test and retention test for all the three groups mentioned in the study. The English version of the final form of achievement test is given in Appendix-V.

Sample Design.

For the purpose of this investigation, 50 slow learners of VIII std from S.S.H.N. Hr. Sec. School, Muhavoor were selected. Out of the 50 slow learners finally selected for the study, two groups were formed following systematic random sampling technique. They were placed in an order of merit. All the odd number students formed the control group while the even number students constituted the experimental group. To see whether both the groups were matched or not, mean and S.D. were calculated for their half yearly exam scores and RPM scores. Then t-test was applied. The obtained t-values (0.62) and (0.78) revealed that both groups were matched ones before the experiment. The control group was taught through traditional lecture method while the experimental group was taught through multimedia based modular approach.

To assess how far this modular approach enables the slow learners to cope with normal students, a normal group comprising average and above average students was also formed. For this group, out of 150 students every sixth student was selected on the basis of systematic random sampling technique. This normal group was also taught through traditional lecture method only.

Data Collection

At the end of the experimental period a post-test was conducted to the slow learners of experimental group, the slow learners of the control group and the students of the normal group. Also, to measure their retention of acquired informations, a retention test was also administered to them after a lapse of two months period. The responses given by the three groups formed the vital data required for the analysis. The scores of the three groups in the pre-test, post-test and retention test are given in Appendix-VIII.

Scoring Procedure

The achievement test consisted of 100 objective type questions. The total score of the test is 100. For each correct answer, the score is 'one'; and for each wrong answer the score is 'zero'. The answer key to the achievement test is given in Appendix-VI. English version of the key of the achievement test is given in Appendix-VII.

Statistical Techniques used in the Study

The data thus obtained were analysed by using appropriate statistical techniques such as Mean, Standard Deviation and t-test.

Findings and Conclusions

An overall analysis reveals the following:

1. There is no significant difference in the pre-test performance between the control group slow learners and the experimental group slow leamers (t-value 0.57). The absence of variation in their pre-test performance bears testimony to the fact that both the control group and the experimental group in the present study were matched ones before the experiment (refer Table-1).
2. There is significant difference between the pre-test performance of control group slow learners and the normal group students (t-value 16.0). Further, the achievement of normal group students is higher than the achievement of control group slow learners (refer Table-2).
3. There is significant difference between the pre-test mean scores of the experimental group slow learners and the normal group students (t-value 14.92). Further, the achievement of normal group students is higher than the achievement of experimental group slow learners (refer Table-3).
4. There is no significant difference between the pre-test and post-test mean scores of the control group slow learners taught through traditional lecture method

(t-value 1.94). Though, their performance was better in the post-test, they could not make significant difference (refer Table-4).

5. There is significant difference between the pre-test and post-test scores of experimental group slow learners when the subjects are taught through multimedia based modular approach (t-value 12.61). Further, their achievement is higher in the post-test than in the pre-test. Moreover, an analysis of rate of progress made by both control group slow learners and the experimental group slow learners throws light on the effectiveness of multimedia based modular approach with special reference to slow learners. From a meagre mean score of 20.6 in the pre-test, the experimental group slow learners could gain an impressive mean score of 46.2 in the post-test which is more than double the pre- test mean score. But, the control group slow learners could not make significant mean gain. This vouchsafes the advantage of multimedia based modular approach over the traditional lecture method (refer Table-5). It conforms to the findings of Gabriel, Pillai and Gnanam (1989), Ramar (1994), Postlethwat, Novah and Murray (1964), Rajaguru (1994) and Schmidt (1991) who all have established that multimedia and modular approach significantly enhanced the achievement of backward students such as low achievers and slow learners after the experimental treatment.

6. There is no significant difference between the pre-test and post-test scores of normal group students when taught through traditional lecture method (t-value 1.96). As in the case of control group, the normal group students also could not make any significant difference in their post-test performance because they could make a mean gain of 4.2 only for 47 (refer Table-6).

7. There is significant difference between the post-test scores of control group slow learners taught through traditional lecture method and the experimental group slow learners taught through multimedia based modular approach (t-value 11.07). Further, the achievement of

the experimental group slow learners is higher than the achievement of control group slow learners (refer Table-7).

In terms of per centage, the rate of progress shown by the experimental group slow learners taught through multimedia based modular approach is 124% (from 20.6 to 46.2) (ref. Table-5), while the rate of progress made by the control group slow learners is 15% (from 19.8 to 22.8) (ref. Table-4). The variation in the rates of progress made by both the groups is the resultant product of multimedia based modular approach and it vouches for the effectiveness of multimedia based modular approach.

8. There is significant difference between the post-test scores of the slow learning boys and the slow learning girls in the control group taught through traditional lecture method (t-value 2.55). From the very meagre mean gain (from 18 to 20.5) made by the slow learning girls in the control group, it is explicit that they could not make as much mean gain as the slow learning boys who made a mean gain of 4 from 20.3 to 24.3. This avers that the traditional lecture method is not effective to the slow learning girls and they need all the more a newer innovative method of instruction to show significant difference in their performance (refer Table 8).

9. Sex has not influenced the post-test performance of the experimental group slow learners as there exists no significant difference between the post-test scores of slow learning boys and slow learning girls in the experimental group (t-value 0 33). While the girls in the matched control group trailed behind the boys, the girls in the experimental group were at par with boys in the post-test performance. This may be attributed to the effectiveness of multimedia based modular approach (refer Table-9).

10. There is significant difference between the post-test scores of the control group slow learners and the normal group students (t-value 14.2). Further, the achievement of the normal group students is higher than the

achievement of control group slow learners (refer Table-10).

The mean values (19.8 and 22.8) obtained by the control group slow learners reveal that though they have made a progress by traditional lecture method, they could not narrow down the gap between them and the normal group students. It means that the traditional lecture method could not enable the control group slow learners to cope with normal students.

11. There is significant difference between the post-test scores of the experimental group slow learners and the normal group students (t-value 2.11). The achievement of normal group students is higher than the achievement of experimental group slow learners (refer Table-11). However, a critical analysis of mean values signifies that the experimental group slow learners significantly improved their achievement after the experiment. Moreover, the multimedia based modular approach enabled the experimental group slow learners to cope with normal students to a great extent. The narrowed down gulf of difference between both the groups bears testimony to the effectiveness of multimedia based modular approach. Further, a comparative study of Table-10 and Table-11 testifies to the advantage of multimedia based modular approach over the traditional lecture method. It is in agreement with the findings of Schmidt (1991), Leitner (1992), Ramar (1994), Reddy and Ramar (1994,1995) and Postlethwat (1964) who have substantiated that CAI, video instruction and modular instruction could enable the backward students like low achievers and slow learners to cope with normal students taught through traditional lecture method.

12. There is no significant difference in the achievements of control group slow learners between the post-test and retention test. It is observed that the mean value has decreased by 0.4. It indicates that the control group slow learners could not remember at the time of retention test all the facts and figures they were aware of at the

time of the post-test. This can be ascribed for the decreased mean value in the retention test. The post-test score is higher than the retention test score in respect of most of the control group slow learners. The mean values of post-test and retention test further suggest that the traditional lecture method could neither contribute to nor promote retention.

13. There is significant difference between the post-test performance and retention test performance of experimental group slow learners. However, the significant mean difference (25.6) between the pre-test and post-test scores of experimental group slow learners highlights the volume of new additional informations acquired by them at the time of post-test. This fast learnt informations could be properly processed in their minds and kept in memory storage even after a period of two months without loss or distortion. This is well testified by the fact that the experimental group slow learners could improve upon their post-test performance in the retention test. Further, it substantiates that the multimedia based modular approach could contribute to and promote retention of slow learners. The better retention of experimental group slow learners is the resultant product of multimedia based modular treatment given to them during the period of experimentation. Also, it strengthens the findings of Hopper (1982) and Rajaguru (1994), Oberai (1981) and Kumar (1981) who have established that multimedia strategy and modular approach very much promote the retention of the students.

14. There is significant difference in the achievements of the normal group students between the post-test and retention test. It is noticed that the mean value has decreased by 0.8. It also indicates that whatever informations they had in their minds at the time of post-test could not be recalled without loss or distortion at the time of retention test. This can be ascribed for their decreased mean value in the retention test. The post-test score is higher than the retention test score for

most of the normal group students. A critical study of the mean values of the post-test and retention test further signifies that the traditional lecture method could neither promote nor facilitate transfer or recall.

15. There is significant difference between the retention test scores of the slow learning boys and the slow learning girls in the control group (t-value 2.27). The achievement of slow learning boys is higher than the achievement of slow learning girls. The difference that was present in the post-test persisted in the retention test also (refer Table-15).

16. There exists no significant difference between the retention test scores of slow learning boys and slow learning girls in the experimental group (t-value 0.21). Both the boys and girls in experimental group have evinced same degree of retention by recalling the facts and concepts already learnt till the post-test at the time of retention test (refer Table-16). The overcrowding of facts and concepts and the rapid acquisition of new informations and concepts during the period of experimentation did not affect their memory storage and retention. The very fact that the slow learners, who are known to be slow to "catch on", have been able to acquire this much of information in a short period and they have been able to retain them in memory for a considerable time, testifies to the effectiveness of multimedia based modular approach. It supports the findings of Madhur Gupta (1989), Oberai (1981), Kumar (1981) and Rajaguru (1994) who have established that multimedia instructional strategy promotes retention of the students.

17. There is significant difference between the pre-test and post-test scores of the experimental group slow learners in English subject (t-value 5.2). Their achievement is higher in the post-test, than in the pre-test. Moreover, the rate of progress made by the experimental group students is higher than the rates of progress made by the other two group students. This fact asseverates the

effectiveness of multimedia based modular treatment (refer Table-17). Also, it supports the findings of Natarajan (1996) who has established effectiveness of modular approach in teaching English

18. There exists significant difference between the pre-test and post-test scores of experimental group slow learners in mathematics subject and their achievement is higher in the post-test than in the pre-test (t-value 5.71). Moreover, the rate of progress made by the experimental group slow learners is more than the rates of progress made by the other two groups. It also implies that multimedia based modular approach is more effective than the traditional lecture method in teaching mathematics to slow learners (refer Table-18). Also, it conforms to the findings of Schram (1965), Maria Araselvi (1996) and Reddy and Ramar (1995) who have signified the effectiveness of video and modular instructions in teaching mathematics subject.

19. There is significant difference between the pre-test and post-test scores of experimental group slow learners in science subject and their achievement is higher in the post-test than in the pre-test (t-value 12.2). Moreover, the rate of progress made by the experimental group slow learners is higher than the rates of progress made by the other two groups (refer Table-19). Also, it is in the science post-test that the experimental group slow learners have surpassed even the normal group students. This performance par excellence of the experimental group slow learners signifies the effectiveness of multimedia based modular approach in teaching science to slow learners and it also testifies to the advantage of multimedia based modular approach over the traditional lecture method in teaching science to slow learners. Also, it supports the findings of Sinnathambi (1991), Madhur Gupta (1989), Basu (1981), Desai (1985), Schram (1965), Chelladurai (1994), Hopper (1992), Thalaimalai (1996) and Reddy and Ramar (1995) who have vouchsafed that video and modular instructions

significantly improved the achievement of students in science after the experimental treatment.

20. There exists significant difference between the pre-test and post-test scores of the experimental group slow learners and their achievement is higher in the post-test than in the pre-test (t-value 8.86). Besides, the rate of progress made by the experimental group slow learners is more than the rates of progress made by the other two groups. The vertical variation in the experimental group slow learners' post-test performance is a sufficient indication to substantiate the effectiveness of multimedia based modular approach in teaching social science to slow learners (refer Table-20). It conforms to the findings of Dhamija (1986), Mahange (1991) and Reddy and Ramar (1995) who have substantiated the effectiveness of modular instruction in teaching social science to normal students as well as backward students.

21. There are significant differences between the pre-test and post-test scores of experimental group slow learners in respect of all the subjects. The highest significant difference is found in science subject with a tremendous mean gain of 43.8 and 171% rate of progress. It is closely followed by social science subject with a mean gain of 28.8 and 133% rate of progress. Trailing behind these two subjects are mathematics and English which have mean gains of 18 and 11.6 and 100% and 64.4% rates of progress respectively. The very fact that the slow learners, who had hitherto no pass mean score in any subject, could now attain pass mean scores in three subjects, is a clear proof beyond doubt for the effectiveness of multimedia based modular approach with special reference to slow learners (refer Table-21).

In terms of media effectiveness, the media effectiveness is more for science subject. The nature of science subject is such that it lends itself for concrete presentation and direct experience in the forms of project work and practicum in the modules. Moreover, video as well as CAI by its power of magnification, can offer a close view of scientific demonstrations to any number of students and it can facilitate teaching of science with animated diagrams. Then comes social science, where the project work and practicum have a bearing on students' achievement. Video can bring social science alive by filmed interviews and case studies of men and women in action in distant places. Also, filming of historical and geographical locations accentuate the learning of slow learners. This brings to light the fact that media effectiveness largely depends on the nature of the subject. English demands active participation of students for a rapid learning. But in this approach, the media are quite active while the students are passive. Also, they need more exposure to true life situations for interaction. The present rate of progress also may be attributed to the interaction ensured in the practicum and project work of the module. Mathematics is a complex subject dealing with abstract concepts. It requires problem solving skill on the part of the learners. Though the multimedia based modular approach could enable the slow learners to show a significant increase in the post test performance in mathematics, it could not bring about the same rate of progress as in science and social science subjects. Hence, mathematics and English, which are complex and hard in nature, naturally trail behind.

In conclusion it may be stated that the experience of this study and a number of others conducted by the researcher in the succeeding years involving the use of similar strategies, which are now included in the second chapter, augments the greater need for practitioner research in the special needs field. Specifically, it will lead the practitioners to understand how educational contexts can be developed in order to foster the learning of all children in the mainstream despite their individual differences or characteristics.

This study encompasses the three perspectives on educational difficulties. It is a research basically carried out by a practitioner. The first perspective seeks to explain educational difficulties in terms of the characteristics of the individual pupils. The frame of reference created by this perspective is the individual child, and responses are chosen that seek to change or support the child in order to facilitate participation in the process of schooling. It allows teacher support system in the context of the regular classroom. Our intervention strategy, that is, multimedia based modular approach facilitates participation of slow learners in the learning process to a considerable extent. Teacher support can be provided in project work as well as follow-up works. This approach is of much value in promoting personalised system of learning in regular mainstream classroom. This caters to individual interest and need. This approach makes use of multimedia in an effective way. The learners can use audio or video or modules in print form according to their own interest and need. It ensures utility of appropriate media and involvement in learning by way of project work and follow-up work. Thus this approach seeks to circumvent educational difficulties in terms of the characteristics of individual pupils.

The second perspective explains educational difficulties in terms of mismatch between the characteristics of particular children and the organisation and/or curriculum arrangements made for them. Responses chosen in the light of this perspective include curriculum adaptations, alternative materials for pupils, or even extra support in the classroom. These are provided for in the multimedia based modular approach. Each unit is divided into three or more conceptual sub-units. Students are supplied with modules for their personal auto learning. The students are provided with additional instructional time and extra support in project works and experiments. As Ainscow has rightly remarked, this will be very beneficial to pupils other than those designated as having special needs. Those who adopt this perspective tend to argue for the use of the term 'individual needs' rather than 'special needs' (Ainscow and Muncey, 1988). The four components of multimedia and modules used in this study very much cater to individual needs in the form of alternative materials.

The third perspective explains educational difficulties in terms of curriculum limitations, using the term curriculum in a broad sense to include all the planned and, indeed, unplanned experiences offered to pupils. Those who adopt this perspective would encourage the idea that additional adults could facilitate the review and development of existing arrangements in the light of a scrutiny of the difficulties experienced by certain pupils. This study probes into the learning difficulties of slow learners and puts forth some suggestions to combat slow learning. This approach ensures better pupil participation and involvement in learning. It ignites spark of interest in pupils and reaches out to all learners. How far it is effective in other setting is yet to be assessed. It is very difficult to work out what works in theory. Such an orientation is fraught with difficulties. On the other hand, the potential benefits are enormous, not least in that the understandings gained may have an immediate impact on the development of thinking and practice.

IMPLICATIONS OF THE STUDY

1. The results of the study have established that multimedia based modular approach is more effective than the traditional lecture method in teaching basic subjects of std VIII to slow learners. When it is very effective to slow learners, it has to be equally effective, if not more effective, to other backward students like under achievers, low achievers etc. Only the degree of efficacy might differ.
2. Identifying slow learners at primary level itself will enable the teachers to devise required remedial instruction to facilitate their learning. The teachers trained in this regard will be able to identify and tackle slow learning at early stage itself.
3. Expertise of resource persons can be utilised for development of modules for various subjects and various standards and thus, their expertise can be made available to a wider range of student population.
4. Teachers of Middle Schools and High Schools can be given orientation as to how to prepare modules and how to develop multimedia packages especially LTIM materials making use of the resources locally available. This will give them a better preparedness to ensure optimum human resource development.

5. Keeping the result of the study in mind, the NCERT and SCERT may take up the onerous task of developing modules for each subject as they produce teachers handbook and these can be supplied to all the schools so that the teachers can effectively make use of these modules, if not for the benefit of the entire class, at least for the benefit of the slow learners, low achievers and under achievers, since the modules, being self contained and auto instructional, cater to individual differences.

6. The instructional video programmes based on subject unit may be developed by the NCERT and SCERT making use of the expertise of talented teachers at national level and state level respectively. These video cassettes may be supplied to all the schools. If it is not possible due to paucity of fund to supply to all the schools, a central library may be set up at district head quarters to lend the cassettes to the aspiring schools. Since almost all the schools have T.V. of their own, it will be very much possible for them to play the cassettes and the students can view the instructional programmes based on their subject units. In this way the expertise of the talented teachers can be made available even to the schools in the remote far flung areas.

7. Video cassettes and audio cassettes based on subject unit can be developed even by commercial agencies and the schools can procure them either from science or from audio visual fund available in the special fees account.

8. The students can take these cassettes home and they can learn according to their convenience at their own rate without any sort of inhibition.

9. CAI and CAL softwares also can be developed by the NCERT and SCERT and even by commercial agencies since they are deemed to be more effective to slow learners, low achievers and under achievers. So the teachers should be adequately prepared by means of orientation programmes to play a supportive role in

order to lead the learners towards optimum level of attainment.

10. Since the computer finds a place in the syllabus of high schools right from class IX onwards, the use of CAI and CAL can be widely popularised without much effort.

11. It is not necessary that a school should buy all these multimedia packages if they don't have adequate fund. One school may buy audio cassettes, another school may purchase video cassettes and yet another school may procure CAI software and these schools can exchange these various multimedia packages among themselves.

12. Since multimedia based modular approach has a far reaching consequence for the backward students, it can be effectively made use of in distance education in which about 50% of the total enrolled students are average and below average. Appropriate and optimum use of media sources will yield better result in distance education. Setting up a separate channel for education will be a landmark in human resource development and ultimately national development. The huge amount spent in this regard should be taken in the right spirit as investment made on education or human capital.

13. With a view to ensure optimum human resource development special remedial classes should be arranged for slow learners in the evening hours as we have special coaching classes for the SC/ST students in the evening hours. In case of SC/ST special coaching classes four teachers for teaching students of standards from VIII to X and eight teachers handling students of standards XI and XII are paid by the state for this special task. In similar manner, the teachers entrusted with the task of remedial coaching for slow learners can also be paid by the state for this special task with a view to optimise human resource development.

14. Since the use of multimedia based modular approach enhances the achievement of slow learners, it will diminish wastage and stagnation in our schools. So the

teachers should be adequately prepared by means of orientation programme and such orientation may be given at DIET level also, so that awareness about multimedia based modular approach can be developed among the primary school teachers also.

LIMITATIONS OF THE STUDY

The limitations of the study are as follows:

1. This study is confined to the slow learners studying in standard VIII of S.S.H.N. Higher Secondary School, Muhavoor.
2. The sample consists of only 50 slow learners selected on the basis of teachers' observation, their performance in RPM and also on the basis of rate of learning.
3. The slow learners identified on the basis of teachers' observation and interaction were not subjected to any intelligence test. They were administered only Standard Progressive Matrices test which was found to be adequate to identify the slow learners.
4. For all the selected subjects, only three units each were included for the study.
5. For English subject, only two units of language items and spoken English covering vowels, diphthongs and consonants were included in the experiment.
6. The experiment was conducted for a period of 45 working days @1 1/2 hours per day.
7. Multimedia packages were developed based on the video shooting done in the classroom where the experiment was actually conducted by making use of the technical expertise available in the district Headquarters. It is to be noted that the institution where the experiment was conducted is located at a remote rural area far from the madding crowd.
8. The CAI software used in the study was also developed by making use of the technical expertise available at district level.

9. As for CAI, each student could not be provided with separate computer and they had to use the available three computers on turn basis.
10. The achievement test used in the study is a teacher made one. Though, the item difficulty and discriminating power for each test item were calculated, the achievement test, as a whole, was not standardised by the investigator.

SUGGESTIONS FOR FURTHER RESEARCH

1. In this study multimedia based modular approach has been found very effective to teach all the subjects of standard VIII except Tamil to the slow learners. To ensure more dependable conclusion the experiments may be conducted on a wide range of schools.
2. A parallel study can be made to find out the effectiveness of multimedia based modular approach at high school and at higher secondary levels.
3. A parallel study can be conducted to find out the effectiveness of multimedia based modular approach with special reference to under achievers
4. A parallel study can be undertaken to assess the effectiveness of multimedia based modular approach with reference to all the students including average and above average students.
5. Four components of multimedia have been included in this study. A separate study may be attempted to assess intermedia effectiveness or to assess the relative effectiveness of each component medium.
6. A correlational study can be done to assess whether there exists any significant relationship between the nature of the subject and media effectiveness.
7. A separate study can be undertaken to assess the effectiveness of multimedia based modular approach with teacher support system (TSS) and without teacher support system.

8. A parallel study can be made covering the full syllabus of a particular subject and internal analysis can be done.
9. A comparative study can be made in rural and urban areas, selecting students from both the areas.
10. A study can be undertaken to assess the attitude of the students and teachers of high school and middle schools towards multimedia based modular approach.
11. A similar study can be carried out in teaching other units of std VIII subjects.
12. A survey can be undertaken to assess the availability of video equipments and training of humanities and science teachers for developing multimedia packages, especially video lessons for the units of different subjects at middle school and high school levels.

BIBLIOGRAPHY

Adebola Adekoya, 1992, 'Uses of Instructional Method and Media Technology in Training of Extension Managers and Supervisors in Nigeria', *Indian journal of Adult Education,* Vol. 53, No. 3

Ainscow M., 1994, "Supporting International Innovation in Teacher Education'. In IN.W. Bradley *et al.,* (Eds). *Enveloping Teachers, Developing Schools,* Fulton, London.

Ainscow M., 1995, 'Education for All: Making it Happen, *Support for Learning* 10(4), 147-157.

Ainscow M., 1997, 'Would it Work in Theory?: Arguments for Practitioner Research in the Special Needs Field'. In C. Clark *et al.,* (Eds), *Theorsing Special Education.* Routledge.

Ainscow M., 1998, "Reaching out to All Learners: Some Lessons from Experience: Keynote Address Made at the International Conference on School Effectiveness and Improvement, Manchester, January, 1998.

Ainscow M., 1998, 'Inclusion and Exclusion in Schools: Listening to Some Hidden Voices: Manchester University, U.K.

Ainscow M., and Hart, S., 1992, "Moving Practice Forward: *Support for Learning, 7(3),* 114-120.

Ainscow M., and Muncey, 1989, "Meeting Individual Needs in the Primary School, Fulton, London.

Aggrawal S.K., 1975, 'A Psychological Study of Academic Under Achievement at Secondary School Level in the State of Rajasthan', in M.B. Buch (Ed.) *Third Survey of Research in Education*, NCERT, New Delhi.

Agrawal A.N., 1982, 'Indian Economy Vikas Publishing House Pvt. Ltd., New Delhi.

Ahuja G.C., and Ahuja P., 1979, 'Demonstration of Audio-visual and Reading Aids to School Students and Testing their Reading Speed in Three Languages—Kannada, Hindi and English', in M.B. Buch (Ed.) *Third Survey of Research in Education*, NCERT New Delhi.

Allan, Jonny Mac., 1985, 'An Analysis of the Perception of Traditional and Long Distance Students Towards Telecourse', in *Dissertation Abstracts International* 46(5), 1225-A

Alten Stanlay R., 1981, 'Audio in Media'. Wadsworth Publishing Co., Belmont, Calif.

Andrews, Kennath & Gerald, 1986, 'A Study of the Effectiveness of instructional Feedback Provided by Interactive Video Disc Instruction', in *Dissertation Abstracts International*, 46(10).

Antonisamy L., 1989, 'A Study of the Effectiveness of Teaching Environmental Concepts to School Dropouts Through Video and Charts'. *Unpublished M. Phil. Dissertation*, Madurai Kamaraj University, Madurai.

Anupama Shah and Sushmita Mandal, 1994, 'Effectiveness of Three Instructional Strategies for Higher Education', *Experiments in Education*, January 1994.

Arthur R. Jenson, 1980 'Bias in Mental Testing'. Methuen and Co. Ltd., London.

Balasubramanian M. and Yoganandam, M., 1994, 'Trained Teacher vs Technology—A Comparative Study for Effectiveness in Improving English Pronunciation', *Journal of Research in Educational Media*, 1994,2(1)25-30.

Baggalcy J.P. and Stephen Duck, 1974, 'Guidelines in ETV Production: Six Experiments', in Tony Bates and John Rabinson (Eds.) *Evaluating Educational Television and Radio*, The Open University Press.

Basker P.J., 1990, 'A Study of Non-Formal Education Programme for Working Children through Video Method'. *Unpublished M. Phil Dissertation*, Madurai Kamaraj University, Madurai.

Basu M.K., 1981, 'Effectiveness of Multimedia Programmed Material in the Teaching of Physics', in M.B. Buch (Eds) *Third Survey of Research in Education*. NCERT, New Delhi.

Beasley J., 1956, 'Slow to Talk'. Bureau of Publications, Teachers College, Columbia University.

Beatty Lamond F., 1979, 'Filmstrips', Educational Technology Publications Inc. Englewood Cliffs, N.J.

Beatty Lamond, F., 1980, 'Motion Pictures'. Educational Technology Publications, Englewood Cliffs, N.J.

Becker IN.J., 1986, 'Instructional Uses of Computers: Reports from the 1985 National Survey', (Issue No. 1) Johns Hopkins University, Centre for Research on Elementary and Middle Schools, Baltimose, Md.

Benaloh, Laurie Blake, 1994, Teachers, Students and Instructional Software: What Works Well When and Why' in *Dissertation Abstracts International*, Volume 54, Number 9, March 1994.

Best, John W., 1977, 'Research in Education'. Prentice Hall of India, New Delhi.

Bhangoo S. and Kaur S., 1989, 'Educational Video Films in Home Science for Rural Women—An Action Experiment', *Media and Technology for Human Resource Development*. July 89 Vol. 1, No. 4, pp. 19-22.

Bhatt, 1992, 'Effectiveness of Three Modes of Teaching Science on Students' Achievements', *Experiments in Education*, March 1992.

Biswal B., 1982, 'Developing Strategies for Effective Utilization of School Broadcast Programmes in Orissa", *Unpublished Ph. D. Thesis*, MSU, Baroda.

Block J.IN. and Anderson L.W., 1975, 'Mastery Learning in Classroom Instruction'. Macmillan, New York.

Block J.IN. and Burns R.B., 1976, 'Mastery Learning; in L.S. Shilman (Ed), *Review of Research in Education*, Vol. 4, Itasca, III: F.E. Peacock.

Bloom B.S., 1976, 'Human Characteristics and School Learning'. McGraw-Hill, New York.

Bob Leempkins *et al.*, 1991, 'Instructional Equity for Low Achievers in Elementary School Mathematics', The *Journal of Educational Research*, 84(3), January-February 1991, Washington D.C., pp. 135-138.

Borg Walter R., 1965, 'Educational Research—An Introduction'. David Makay Company, Inc., New York.

Borras Isabel, 1994, 'Effects of subtitled Video during Transactional Task Practice on Oral Communicative performance of Fifth Semester College Students of French Learning with Multimedia Course Ware', in *Dissertation Abstracts International*, Vol. 54, No. 8, Feb., 1994.

Broyles, Pamela, 1986, 'Influence of Video Tape Feedback on Students' and Teachers' Reaction of Public Speaking Performance', in *Dissertation Abstracts International* 46 (12) 3693-A.

Burt C., 1942, The Backward Child'. U.L.P., 2nd Edition, 1946, London.

Butts and Prickets, 1969, 'Comparison in the Effectiveness of Tape Slide Materials in Audio-Tutorial Laboratories and Conventional Teaching', in Mullick 1985 *Strategies of Programmed, Instruction'*, Sunday Press, New Delhi.

Cabeceiras James, 1981, 'The Multimedia Library Materials Selection and Use: Academic Press, New York.

Carbo *et al.*, 1986, 'Teaching Students to Read Through Their Individual Learning Styles', Englewood Cliffs, Prentice Hall, New Jersey.

Chanda A.K., 1966, 'Report of the Committee on Broadcasting and Information Media', New Delhi, Govt. of India.

Chandhari, V.P. Jain, 1975, 'Factors Contributing to Academic Under Achievement', in M.B. Buch (Ed) *Third Survey of Research in Education*, NCERT, New Delhi.

Chelladurai N., 1994, 'Impact of Modular Approach on Developing Environmental Awareness Among Primary Students'. *Unpublished M. Phil* Dissertation. Alagappa University, Karaikudi.

Chintamani Kar, 1992, 'Exceptional Children—Their Psychology and Instruction'. Sterling Publishers Private Ltd., New Delhi.

Choatm E., *et al.* 1986, 'Educational Television and Curriculum for Children upto the Age of Seven Years', in *British Journal of Educational Technology* Vol. 17 (3), London: Council for Educational Technology.

Clark, Kenneth F., 1987 'Interactive Video Training of Preservice Teachers in Domain TV of the Florida Performance Measurement System', in *Dissertation Abstracts International*, 46(10).

Cleugh M.F., 1957, 'The Slow Learner" Methuen, 1957.

Coleman *et al.*, 1966, 'Equality of Educational Opportunity; Department of Health, Education and Welfare, Washington, D.C.

Comstock George, 1980, ''Television in America; Sage Publishing, Beverly Hills, Calif.

Corno L. and Snow R.E., 1986, 'Adapting Teaching to Individual Differences Among Learners' in M.C. Wittrock (Ed.) *Handbook of Research of Teaching* (3rd Ed.) Macmillan, New York.

Cox, R.A., The Process of Educational Technology, A Tool for Development'. Mac-Millan Company, London, p. 58.

Curtis K. and Shaver J.P., 1980, 'Slow Learners and the Study of Contemporary Problems', Social Education, 44, 4, pp. 302-38, April.

Das R.C., 1993, 'Educational Technology—A Basic Text'. Sterling Publishers Private Ltd., New Delhi.

Davies I.K. and James Hartly, 1976, 'Contribution of Educational Technology', Mc-Graw Hill Book Company, London, p. 490.

Davis I.K., 1973, 'Effectiveness of a Tape Slide Unit on the Radio Telephone, Third Class License with Broadcast Endorsement Against the Conventional Approach, Which Involved Teachers and Demonstration', in M.B. Buch (Ed.) *Second Survey of Research in Education,* NCERT, New Delhi.

Deka U., 1985, 'A Causal Comparative study of High and Low Achievers', in M.B. Buch (Ed.) *Fourth Survey of Research in Education,* NCERT, New Delhi.

Desai K.V., 1985, 'An Investigation into the Efficiency of Different Instructional Media in the Teaching of Science to the Pupils of Class VIII in Relation to Certain Variables'. *Ph.D. Thesis in Education,* M.S. University, Baroda.

Dhamija N., 1985, 'Effectiveness of Three Approaches of Instruction Conventional, Radio Vision and Modular Approach on Achievement of Students in Social Studies', in M.B. Buch (Ed.) *Fourth Survey of Research in Education.*

Dobbin E., Renee, 1994, 'Math Computer - assisted Instruction with Remedial Students and Students with Mild Learning/Behavioural disabilities', in *Dissertation Abstracts International,* Volume 54, No. 8, February 1994.

Doneriya A., 1988, 'A Study of General Educational Television Programme in Terms of their Contents, Presentations and Students' Reactions and Effectiveness'. Unpublished M. Ed dissertation, DAVV, Indore.

Duncan J., 1942, 'The Education of the Ordinary Child'. Nelson.

Dunn R.S. and Dunn K.J., 1978, 'Teaching Students Through Their Individual Learning Styles: A Practical Approach". Reston, Va: Reston.

Edward Sahaya Raj, 1994, 'Effectiveness of Lecture Method Supplemented with Low Cost Teaching Aids in Learning Physics'. *Unpublished M. Phil Dissertation*, Alagappa University, Karaikudi.

Elmore, Patricia Venshew, 1992, 'An Analysis of Fifty One Computer Modules Designed to Enhance the Knowledge, Skills and Attitude Needed by Teacher Education Students', in *Dissertation Abstracts International,* Vol. 52, Numbers February, 1992.

Foxall A. and Tom Evans, 1973, 'Closed-Circuit Television for Teaching in Further Educational Institutions', in Derick Unwing (Ed.) *Programmed Learning and Educational Technology,* Volume 10, London Sweet and Maxwell, pp. 170-180.

Gabriel, J.P., Pillai, J.K. Gnanam, 1989, 'Modularisation-An Attempt at Collegiate Level in India', *Media and Technology for Human Resource Development,* January, 1985.

Gagne R.M., 1983, 'Is Educational Technology in Phase?' Journal of Educational Technology, Vol. 20, No. 2, pp. 7-14.

George, A., 1966, 'An Enquiry into the Scope and Effectiveness of Audio-Visual Instruction in Improving English Teaching in Kerala State in the First Years of School Course' in M.B. Buch (Ed.), *Second Survey of Research in Education,* Baroda, C.A.S.E., M.S. University, 1974.

Gerald IN., 1977, 'Teaching Slow Learners'. Temple Smith, London.

Ghosh A.K., 1996, 'Human Resource Development', in University News, Monday, January, 15, 1996.

Ghuman M.S., 1976, 'A Study of Aptitude, Personality Traits and Achievement Motivation of Academic Over Achievers and Under Achievers', in M.B. Buch (Ed.) *Third Survey of Research in Education,* NCERT, New Delhi.

Girija Devi, Thampuratty, 1995, 'Socio-Economic Status of Creative High Achievers and Creative Low Achievers in Mathematics', *Experiments in Education* Vol. XVIII, No. 5, pp. 93-97.

Golani T.P., 1982, "The Use of Audio-visual Aids in the Secondary Schools of District Thane', in M.B. Buch (Ed.), *Third Survey of Research in Education,* 1978-83, NCERT, New Delhi.

Good, Barr and Scales, 1935, 'Methodology of Educational Research'. Appleton Century Crofts, Inc. New York.

Heinich Robert, 1970, 'Technology and the Management of Instruction'. Association for Educational Communications and Technology, Washington, D.C

Hiaman and Purushothaman, 1988, 'Instruction through Interactive Video", in M.B. Buch (Ed.) *4th Survey of Research in Education,* NCERT, New Delhi.

Hiaman and Purushothaman, 1991, 'Effectiveness of Educational Television', Paper Presented in AIAET Annual Conference, Bhubaneswer, 27, Dec., 1991.

Himmelweit IN., *et al.*, 1958, 'Television and the Child', London Nufield Foundation, London.

Holtzman W.IN. and Isabel R.L., 1981, 'Impact of Educational Television on Young Children in India', Paris, UNESCO.

Hopper W.A.P., 1982, 'An Experimental Study in the use of Modular Approach for Teaching Biology in Std XI, in M.B. Buch (Ed.) *Third Survey of Research in Education,* NCERT, New Delhi.

Idayavani, 1991, 'Developing a Video Programme on Weathering and Work of the Rivers in Physical Geography for Higher

Secondary Students'. *Unpublished M. Phil. Dissertation*, Madurai Kamaraj University, Madurai.

Ingram C., 1953, The Education of Slow Learning Child', Harrap.

Iyer K.K., 1977, 'Some Factors Related to under Achievement in Maths of Secondary School Students', in M.B. Buch (Ed.) *Third Survey of Research in Education*, NCERT, New Delhi.

Jaiswal K., 1988, 'A Study of Science ETV programmes in Terms of their Contents, Presentations. Students' Reactions and Effectiveness', Unpublished M. Ed. Dissertation, D A V V, Indore.

James Brown, *et al.*, 1985, 'AV Instruction' (Technology, Media and Methods). McGraw Hill Book Co., Singapore.

Janucik R., 1977, Television Agricultural Secondary School in Poland', in Tomy Bates and John Robinsion (Eds.) *'Evaluating Educational Television and Radio'*, The Open University Press.

Jayachandran J., 1980. The Efficacy of Programmed Film Strips for Teaching History to Secondary School Children', in M.B. Buch (Ed.) *Third Survey of Research in Education*, 1978-83, NCERT, New Delhi.

Jayalakshmi R., 1992, "Developing a Video Programme and its Effectiveness in Teaching Balanced Diet to Hr. Secondary Home Science Students and Community People'. *Unpublished M. Phil Dissertation*, Alagappa University, Karaikudi.

Jayalakshmi T.K., 1985 'Systematising Instructional Modules in Educational Psychology at B. Ed., Level", in M.B. Buch (Ed.) *Fourth Survey of Research in Education*, NCERT, New Delhi.

John P. De. Cecco, 1988. The Psychology of Learning and Instruction". Printice Hall of India Private Ltd., New Delhi.

Jowett, Garth, and James M. Linton, 1980, "Movies as mass Communication". Sage Publications, Beverly Hills, Calif.

Kalimuthu T., 1991, 'Developing a Video Programme on Environmental Pollution in Biology for Higher Secondary Students'. *Unpublished M. Phil Dissertation,* Madurai Kamaraj University, Madurai

Kanade IN.M., 1982, 'A Study of the Impact of ITV on Behaviour of Rural Elementary School Children'. *Unpublished Ph.D. Thesis, M.S. University,* Baroda.

Kamp, Jerrold E., 1980. 'Planning and Producing Audio Visual Materials'. Haper and Row, New York.

Kanna R., 1977, The Impact of Farmer's Television Programme in Athupakkam Village'. *Unpublished M. Phil. Dissertation,* University of Madras, Madras.

Kaplan Don, 1980, 'Video in the Classroom, A guide to Creative Television'. Knowledge Industry Publications, White Plains, N.Y.

Karpaga Kumaravel, 1988, 'Comparing the Effectiveness of Video Assisted Instruction over the Conventional Method of Teaching English'. *Unpublished M. Phil. Dissertation,* Madurai Kamaraj University, Madurai.

Kaur R. and Koshy, *et al.,*., 1970, 'Impact of Television on Farm Women'. M.Sc., Dissertation, I.A.R.I. Delhi.

Khan S.A., 1983, 'A Study of Personality Characteristics of Educationally Backward Pupils of Hr. Sec. Schools of Lucknow District'. *Unpublished Ph.D. Thesis.* Avadh University.

Kirk S.A., 1940, 'Teaching Reading to Slow Learning Children'. Houghton Mifflin.

Koul L., 1978, 'Personality Needs of High and Low Achievers in Maths' in M.B. Buch (Ed.) *Third Survey of Research in Education,* NCERT, New Delhi.

Kour R., 1981, 'An Enquiry into the Effectiveness of Self Instructional Audio Cassettes in Developing Teaching Skills Among Student Teachers', *Unpublished Ph. D. Thesis,* Punjab University.

Kumar A., 1981, 'The Effectiveness of Self-Instructional Audio-Cassettes in Developing Teaching Skills Among Student Teachers in a Three Phased Study', in M.B. Buch (Ed.) *Third Survey of Research in Education,* NCERT, New Delhi.

Kumar A., 1981, 'An Experimental Study of the Relative Effectiveness of Three Methods of Instruction Exposition Method, Programmed Learning Method' and Multi-Media Method in Science Education', in M.B. Buch (Ed.) *Third Survey of Research in Education,* NCERT, New Delhi.

Kumaraiah, 1976, "Intellectual, Personal and Social Factors Related to High and Low Achievement of Various Stages in Medical Education', Ph. D. Thesis in M.B. Buch (Ed.) *Second Survey of Research in Education,* NCERT, New Delhi.

Kwan, Shang Ram Micheel, 1986, 'The Development of an Interactive Video Programme in a Secondary School", in *Dissertation Abstracts International,* 46(3) 2272.

Lalit Mohan Mathur, 1990, 'Planning, Producing and Presenting Inexpensive Instructional Materials and Devices'. International Educational Research Centre, New Delhi.

Lalit Mohan Mathur, 1990, 'Individualised Teaching Learning Manual-Methods, Techniques and Strategies'. International Educational Research Centre, Delhi.

Lee IN.R., 1970, 'Are We Ready for Satellite Television?' Vidura, Vol. 7, pp. 48-55.

Leitner, Rone Karan, 1992, "Comparing the Effects on Reading Comprehension of Educational Video, Direct Experience and Print', in *Dissertation Abstracts International,* Volume 53, Number 3, September 1992.

Luisa Livia, 1991, 'A Study of the Effects of Technology training on Teacher Productivity and Empowerment', in *Dissertation Abstracts international,* Vol. 52, Number 1, July, 1991.

Mahajan S., 1992, 'Development of Computer Software for Automation of the Diploma Course in Computer Education', *Unpublished Ph. D. Thesis,* DAVV, Indore.

Mahony, Sheila, *et al.*, 1980, 'Keeping up with the New Television Public Television and Changing Technology, (ED 192 721), ERIC, Washington, D.C.

Mallick P. and Sahoo, P.K. 1994, 'Effectiveness of School Level ETV Programme with and without Talk Back Facilities in Terms of Achievement of Rural Background students', in *Educational Media* 1994, 2(1)33-44.

Maria, Araselvi S., 1996, "Effectiveness of Audio and Video Cassettes in Teaching Maths at Secondary Level'. *Unpublished M. Phil. Dissertation,* Madurai Kamaraj University, Madurai.

Mathur S.K., 1990, '400 Experiments, Demonstrations and Models in Science with Associated Science Projects', 'New Focuses on Teaching Learning and Remembering a Lesson', 'Classroom Science Activities and Teacher Demonstration Manual', International Educational Research Centre, New Delhi.

Mclean, Loise Maxine, 1986, 'Seeking Information Interactive Video—The Information Sources and Strategy Used by Corporate Training Developer', in *Dissertation Abstracts International,* 46 (12), 3695.

Minor Ed., 1978, 'Handbook for Preparing Visual Media'. Mcgraw-Hill Book Company, New York.

Mishra S.P., 1979, 'A Comparative Study of High and Low Achievers in Science, Commerce and Arts on Creativity Intelligence and Anxiety', in M.B. Buch (Ed.) *Third Survey of Research in Education,* NCERT, New Delhi.

Misra S.K., and Puri, V.K., 1991, 'Economics of Growth and Development". Himalaya Publishing House, Delhi.

Mody B., 1979, 'Programming for SITE', *Journal of Communication',* Vol. 29 (4), pp. 90-98.

Mukhopadhyay, 1981, 'Micro Teaching Versus Modular Approach—Comparative Effectiveness in Developing Teaching Competence', in M.B. Buch (Ed.) *Third Survey of Research in Education,* NCERT, New Delhi.

Mullick S.P., 1981, 'Development of Learning Materials for Non-Formal Education of Girls in Rural Areas', in M.B. Buch (Ed.) *Third Survey of Research in Education,* NCERT, New Delhi.

Naggy, Linda Farinclli, 1992, 'The Introduction of Interactive Video into the Secondary Science Curriculum: A Case Study Using an Instruction Design Model', in *Dissertation Abstracts International,* Volume 52, Number?, January 1992.

Natarajan N., 1994, 'Effectiveness of Modular Approach in Learning English by the Plus Two Hr. Sec. Students'. *Unpublished M. Phil. Dissertation,* M.K. University, Madurai.

Nishino, Alan Koki, 1994, 'An Exploratory Investigation to Determine the Effects of a Multimedia Computer Based Science Learning Environment and Gender Differences on Achievement and Attitudes and Interests of Students in an Eighth Grade Science Classroom', in *Dissertation Abstracts International,* Volume 54, Number 12, June, 1994.

Oberai N., 1985, 'Development and Evaluation of Radio Vision as an Instructional System'. *Unpublished Ph. D.* Thesis, Meerut University.

Oliver J.N., 1956, 'Physical Education of ESN Children'. *Educational Review Volume,* VIII, Number, 2, 1956.

Onah 1970, In Mullick, S.P. (1985), 'Strategies in Programmed Instruction', New Delhi Sunday Press.

Osuala C.E., 1984, 'Educational Technology in Africa: In Reddy (Ed.) Curriculum Development and Educational Technology'. Sterling Publishers Pvt. Ltd.; New Delhi.

Paivio A., 1991, 'Imagery and Verbal Processes'. Nolt, New York.

Patki S.D., 1989, 'Place of Charts in Teaching Learning Process', *Media and Technology For Human Resource Development,* Vol. 1, No. 2.

Peterson, J., 1989, 'Remediation is no Remedy', *Educational Leadership,* 46(6) pp 24-25.

Phutela, R.L., 1980, 'Study into Utilization and Comprehensibility of School Television Programme in Delhi', NCERT, New Delhi.

Pillai, G.S., 1988, 'Appropriate Instructional Media Selection in India', *Media and Technology for Human Resource Development.* Vol. 1, No. 1.

Postlethwart, S.N. Novak, J., 1964, 'An Integrated Experience Approach to Learning' in Volume 6 of *Encyclopaedia of Education,* Mc and The Free Press, U.S.A.

Prasanna, K.C.B., 1984, 'A Study of Certain Mental Health Variables Associated with High and Low Achieving Adolescents', *Ph.D. Education Thesis,* Kerala University.

Pringle and Bassio, 1958, 'A Study of Deprived Children', Part 2, Vita Humana, Vol. 1, 1958.

Priti Dube, V.K. Swarnkar and S.K. Dube, 1990, 'Instructional Television Programmes on Household and Family Planning Practices of Women', *Media and Technology for Human Research Development,* October 1990 Vol. 3, No. 1.

Pushpita John, 1977, 'Some Socio-Personal Attitudes Related to High and Low Academic Performance of Secondary School Leavers', Ph.D. Thesis, in M.B. Buch (Ed.) *Second Survey of Research in Education,* NCERT, New Delhi.

Rai P.N., 1974, 'A Comparative Study of a few Differential Personality Correlates of Low and High Achievers' Ph.D. Thesis, in M.B. Buch (Ed.) *Second Survey of Research in Education,* NCERT, New Delhi.

Rajeswari C. and Mohan, 1996, 'Developing Multimedia Instructional Strategy, Selection, Consolidation, Validation (Part I and II)', *Journal of Research in Educational Media.* January 1996, Volume 3, Number 1.

Ramar R., 1994, 'Effectiveness of Multimedia Based Modular Approach with Special Reference to Low Achievers', *Unpublished M. Phil Dissertation,* Alagappa University, Karaikudi.

Ramend Das Gupta, 1989, 'A Study Aimed at Comparing the PSI with Conventional Method for Technological Curriculum on a more Rigorous Basis and Collecting of Detailed Feedback from the Technology Students', in M.B. Buch (Ed.) *Fourth Survey of Research in Education,* NCERT, New Delhi.

Ramesh C. Sharma, 1993, 'Effect of Four Classroom Presentation Modes on the Achievement of Secondary Students in Science'. *Media and Technology for Human Resource Development,* July 93, Vol. 5, No. 4

Rao K.R., 1981, 'A Comparative Study of Relative Effectiveness of Four Methods of Teaching Literacy to Adiuts', in M.B. Buch (Ed.) *Third Survey of Research in Education,* NCERT, New Delhi.

Ravindranath M.J., 1982 'Development of Multimedia Instructional Strategy for Teaching Science at Secondary level', in M.B. Buch (Ed.) Third *Second Survey of Research in Education,* NCERT, New Delhi.

Ravindranath M.J., 1989, "On the Use of Computers in the Teaching of Environmental Education', in M. B. Buch (Ed.) *Fourth Survey of Research in Education,* NCERT, New Delhi.

Ramachandran K.T., 1982, 'A study of Use of Visual Aids by Teachers of University of Agricultural Sciences', in M.B. Buch (Ed.) *Third Survey of Research in Education.* NCERT, New Delhi.

Reddy and Ramar, 1994, Effectiveness of Multimedia Based Modular Approach in Teaching Social Science to Low Achievers' Media and Technology for Human Resource Development, Vol. 6, No. 3, April-June 1994.

Reddy and Ramar, 1995, 'Effectiveness of Multimedia Based Modular Approach in Teaching Science to Low Achievers'. Journal of Research in Educational Media Vol. 2, No. 2, January 1995.

Reddy and Ramar, 1995, 'Effectiveness of Multimedia Based Modular Approach in Teaching Maths to Low Achievers' Journal of Higher Education, U.G.C., Vol. 18. No. 2, January, 1995.

Reddy and Ramar, 1995, 'Effectiveness of CAI in Teaching Science to Slow Learners'. In *Slow Learners: Their Psychology and Instruction.* Discovery Publishing House, New Delhi, India.

eddy and Ramar, 1996a, 'Relative Effectiveness of Video Instruction in Teaching Science and Social Science to Slow Learners: Paper presented at the Third National Conference on Development of Educational Technology, ?arathithaean University, Dec. 27,28,1996.

Reddy a. l Ramar, 1996b, 'Identifying Slow Learners'. *I.C.C.W. Jou nal, July-Dec.,* 1996.

Reddy and Ramar, 1997a, 'Effectiveness of Multimedia Based Modular Approach in Teaching English to Slow Learners'. Disabilities and Impairments, Vol 11(1), 1997, 3344.

Reddy and Ramar, 1997b, 'Effectiveness of Multimedia Instructional Strategy in Teaching Science to Slow Learners. Journal of Indian Education, Aug. '97.

Reddy and Ramar, 1997c, 'Impact of Modular Approach on Achievement of Slow Learners in Mathematics'. In Slow Learners: *Their Psychology and Instruction.* Discovery Publishing House, New Delhi, India.

Reddy, Ramar and Kusuma, 1997, 'Slow Learners'. Their Psychology and Instruction'. Discovery Publishing House, New Delhi, India.

Reddy, Usha and Vyasula, 1987, Television in Higher Education: the Indian Experience'. Media in Education and Development, pp. 128-133.

Regser, Gail Renee, 1991, 'Effects of Computer Education on Students' Achievement, Attitude and Self Esteem', in Dissertation Abstracts International, Volume 52, No. 1, July, 1991.

Rita Chopra, 1992, 'Effects of Teaching Modules or Achievement Scores of Male and Female Adults', Indian Journal of Adult Education, Volume 53, Number 3, 1992.

Robert Michael, R., 1994 'A Comparison in the Effectiveness of the Delivery of an Interactive Computer-assisted Instruction Module to a Traditional Lecture/Lab Delivered Module', in *Dissertation Abstracts International*, Vol. 54, Number 11, May, 1994.

Robert Slavin, 1985, 'Educational Psychology—Theory into Practice'. Printice Hall of India, Private Ltd., New Delhi.

Russell James, D. and Kathleen, A. Johanningsmeier, 1981, 'Improving Competence Through Modular Instruction', Kendall/Hunt, Dubuque, Iowa.

Sahajahan M.M., 1980, 'An Experimental Study of Teaching Science in Stds VI and VII Through Modules', in M.B. Buch (Ed.) *Third Survey of Research in Education*, NCERT, New Delhi.

Sastry 1982, 'Comparing the Effectiveness of Toys/Models and Figures to Teach Children Over the Conventional Lecture Metnod of Teaching', in M.B. Buch (Ed.) *Third Survey of Research in Education*, NCERT, New Delhi.

Satwant Bhangoo and Amrit Kaur, 1995, 'An Experimental Study of the Multimedia Approach in Learning by Adult Rural Women', Indian Journal of Adult Education Volume 56, Number 1, Jan.-March, 1995

Saun G.S., 1980, 'Patterns of Self Disclosures and Adjustment Among High and Low Achievers', in M.B. Buch (Ed.) *Third Survey of Research in Education*, NCERT, New Delhi.

Schmidt, Susan Carol, 1992, Technology for the 21st Century: The Effects of an Integrated Distributive Computer Network System on Student Achievement', in *Dissertation Abstracts International*, Volume 52, Number 7, January 1992.

Schramm W., 1965, 'Comparing Educational or Instructional Television with Conventional Classroom Teaching in Schools and Colleges', Washington, D. C., Academy for Educational Development.

Schramm Wilber and Godwin C. Chu, 1979, 'Learning From Television', National Association of Educational Broadcasters, Washington, D.C.

Selvaraj M., 1992, 'Role of Mass Media in Creating Population Awareness Among Rural People in Sakkottai Block'. *Unpublished M. Phil Dissertation*, Alagappa University, Karaikudi.

Seth I., 1983, A Study of Effectiveness of Education Television on the Educational Development of Primary School Children'. *Unpublished Ph.D.* Thesis. Baroda.

Sethi A.S., 1976, 'A Study of a Programme in English Spelling in Relation to Visual and Auditory Presentation', in M.B. Buch (Ed.) *Second Survey of Research in Education*, NCERT, New Delhi.

Shah S.G., 1979, 'Development and Try-out of Multi-Media Package on Effective Questioning in the Context of Micro Teaching", in M. B. Buch (Ed.) *Third Survey of Research in Education*, NCERT, New Delhi.

Shah A. and Gupta, S., 1986, 'Effectiveness of Visual Aid; Comparative Study', *Indian Journal of Adult Education*, Vol. 47(6).

Singh A.D., 1983, 'A Comparative Study of High an Achievers in Self Concept Formation', in M. B. Buch (Ed.) *Fourth Survey of Research in Education,* NCERT, New Delhi

Singh B., 1986, 'A Study of Some Possible Contributing Factors to High and Low Achievement in Mathematics of the High School Students of Orissa', in M.B. Buch (Ed.) *Fourth Survey of Research in Education,* NCERT, New Delhi.

Singh I.N., 1984, 'A Survey of Study Habits of High, Middle and Low Achiever Students in Relation to Their Sex, Intelligence and Socio Economic Status', in M.B. Buch (Ed.) *Fourth Survey of Research in Education.* NCERT, New Delhi

Singh K.K., 1985, 'Some Personality Factors of High and Low Intelligent Boys and Girls of Bhagalpur, *Ph.D. (Psychology) Thesis,* Bhagalpur University.

Singh and Shukla, 1986, A Case Study of School Broadcast in Delhi, CET, NCERT, New Delhi, 1980.

Singhal A. *et al.*, 1988, 'The Discussion of Television in India', Media Asia. Vol. 5(4), pp. 222-229.

Sinnathambi V., 1991, 'Developing a Video Programme on Energetics in Chemistry for Higher Secondary Students'. *Unpublished M. Phil. Dissertation,* Madurai Kamaraj University, Madurai.

Slavin Robert, 1988, 'Synthesis of Research Grouping in Elementary and Secondary Schools'. *Educational Leadership* 46(1), pp 67-77.

Smart Leathy Ann, 1994, The Effect of Traditional Versus Multimedia Augmented Instruction on Exposure Time Determination', in *Dissertation Abstracts International*, Volume 54, Number 10, April 1994.

Smith Bonie Jean, 1994, 'Implementation of Satellite Distance Learning in Illinois Rural Secondary Schools: A Descriptive Study', in *Dissertation Abstracts International,* Volume 54, No. 8, February 1994.

Snow R.E., 1986, 'Individual Differences and the Design of Educational Programs', *American Psychologist*, 41, 1029-1039.

Somasundaram, M., 1980, 'A Comparative Study of Certain Personality Variables Related to over, Normal and Under Achievement in Secondary School Mathematics', in M.B. Buch (Ed.) *Third Survey of Research in Education*, NCERT, New Delhi.

Sontakey V.V., 1986, 'A Comparative Study of Personality Factors and Achievement Motivation of High and Low Achievers in Natural and Biological Science', in M. B. Buch (Ed.) *Fourth Survey of Research in Education*, NCERT, New Delhi.

Soulier J. Steven, 1980, 'Real Objects and Models'. Educational Technology Publications, Englewood, Cliffs, N.J.

Soundararaja Rao and Rajaguru, 1995 'Effectiveness of Video Assisted Instruction on the Achievement of Slow Learners', in *Journal of Educational Research and Extension*, Vol. 32, No. 2, October 1995.

Stanley Ahmann, 1965, 'Testing Student Achievement and Aptitudes'. Prentice-Hall of India (Private) Ltd., New Delhi.

Stule, Jerry Reed, 1994, 'Bridging Distances to the Individual Learner: The Converging of Video, Voice and Data Technologies, in *Dissertation Abstracts International*, Volume 55, Number 2, August 1994.

Stella, 1993, 'Effectiveness of Computer Assisted Instruction with Special Reference to Under Achievers', *Media and Technology for Human Resource Development*, April, 1993, Vol. 5, No 3.

Stirbravy, John, A., 1988, 'Military Students' Attitude towards Classroom Use of Instructional Television at the USAF Academy', in *Dissertation Abstracts International*, 45 (II) 3330-4.

Subramania Pillai. G., 1991, "Instructional Designing-Information on Instructional Technology', Nirmal, Madurai.

Subramanian, S., 1982, 'The Effectiveness of Two Different Methods of Teaching Reading in Primary School", *Journal of Educational Research and Extension*, Vol. 18(3).

Subramanian, S. and Ramadevi, M., 1991, 'Some Differential Characteristics of High and Low Achievers in Secondary Schools', in *Experiments in Education*. Vol. XIX, No 8, August 1991.

Sudame G.R. and Goel D.R., 1988, A Study of School Broadcasts in Baroda, CASE, M.S. University, Baroda.

Sumangala V., 1995, 'Some Psychological Variables Discriminating Between High and Low Achievers', in *Experiments in Education*, Vol. XXIII, Nos 10 & 11, pp 165-175.

Sumitra Ray and Poonam Kumari, 1991, 'Effectiveness of Design Element of Flash Cards for Nutrition Education', *Doctoral Dissertation in Education*, Punjab Agricultural University, Ludhiana.

Swain Dwight, V., 1981, 'Scripting for Video and Audio Visual Media", Focal Press, New York.

Tansley and Gulliford, 1962, 'The Education of Slow Learning Children'. Routeledge and Kegan Paul, London.

Tay, Young-Wu, 1994, 'An Assessment of the Developmental Status of Educational Technology in the People's Republic of China' in *Dissertation Abstracts International*, Volume 54, Number 4, March, 1994.

Tayler, Neil and, 1979, 'Seeing and Perceiving, Films in a World of Change'. Centre for Advanced TV Studies, London, England.

Temyankaran McDonald, 1994, 'Learner Controlled Lessons in Co-operative Learning Groups During Computer Based Instruction', in *Dissertation Abstracts International*, Volume 54, Number 12, June, 1994.

Thalaimalai, R., 1996, 'Effectiveness of Multimedia Based Modular Approach in Teaching Botany at Higher Secondary Level'. *Unpublished M. Phil. Dissertation,* Madurai Kamaraj University, Madurai.

Thomson G.IN., *et al.*, 1947 'The Trend of Scottish Intelligence'. U.L.P., 1947.

Tobias S., 1981 'Adaptation to Individual Differences', in F.IN. Farley and N.J. Gordon (Eds.) Psychology and Education: The state of the Union (pp 60-81) Berkeley, Calif:

Uma Joshi and Anjali Gupta, 1993, "Effectiveness of Video in Educating Women of Low Socio-economic Status', in *Media and Technology for Human Resource Development,* Vol. 5, No 3, April, 1993.

Unwin 1968, Technology of Teaching'. Loyal Book Depot, Meerut.

Vardhini 1983, 'Effectiveness of Multimedia Instructional Strategy in teaching Science (Physics and Chemistry)', in M.B. Buch (Ed.) *Fourth Survey of Research in Education,* NCERT, New Delhi.

Vibha Joshi, 1993, 'Effectiveness of School Television Programme in Science" *Media and Technology for Human Resource Development* Vol. 5, No 2, January, 1993.

Wilkinson, Gene, 1980, 'Media in instruction 60 Years of Research'. Association for Educational Communications and Technology, Washington D.C.

Winter, Christina Surrency 1994, 'A Strategy for Identifying When Interventions Should Occur in Computer assisted Instruction', in *Dissertation Abstracts International,* Volume 55, Number 4, October, 1994.

Yadav, 1982, 'An Experimental Study of Effectiveness of Lecture and Guided Discussion Methods in Developing Hierarchy of Learning Cognitive Domain', in M.B. Buch (Ed.) *Third Survey of Research in Education,* NCERT, New Delhi.

Index

D

E

F

G

H

I

J

K

L

M

N